Preemptive Behavior Therapy

The Path to Self-Correction

Debbie Cowan-Hackett

Russ Hudson

Cover art by Kevin Lacoste

Copyright © 2015 Cowan-Hackett/Hudson

All rights reserved.

ISBN: 0986357103
ISBN-13: 978-0-9863571-0-7

DEDICATION

This book is dedicated to the little ones; the children and creatures who depend on us to help them become bright, healthy beings.

CONTENTS

	Introduction	i
1	Foundations	1
2	Why the Old Ways are Dying	Pg 13
3	Body Language & The Flicker	Pg 23
4	Redirection	Pg 46
5	Correction	Pg 60
6	Reward	Pg 75
7	Clinical vs. Home Application	Pg 92
8	Retraining You	Pg 99
9	Resources	Pg 127
10	Dual Faceted Perspective	Pg 136

INTRODUCTION

Preemptive Behavior Therapy is a guided process that teaches self-correction at the instinctual level, *before* undesired behaviors occur. It's not a term that I coined as part of some outlandish new-fangled method of parenting or teaching. In fact, PBT is actually based on a learning model that is perhaps one of the oldest known: learning through observation of other species. By studying the body language and other behaviors of predators, prey and other animals like our neighbors, Mr. & Mrs. Everyman, we can make accurate predictions about what an individual or even a group might do next.

If the outcome of the impending behavior is productive and desirable, the behavior can be encouraged and reinforced. If the outcome is negative or undesirable, the behavior can be discouraged and corrected.

Preemptive Behavior Therapy takes this one critical step further: instead of correcting negative behaviors, it corrects the thinking and precursors that precede them and thereby prevents the behavior from occurring at all. Similar to the idea behind preventative medicine, PBT seeks to prevent the cause of a behavior as opposed to correcting a behavior that has already occurred.

Animals have taught us a great deal about human behavior, and a majority of the framework for PBT is derived from my work with animals. For thousands of years man has studied his natural environment and mimicked it with much success, but when it comes to our own behaviors - and especially those of our children - we are still undeniably animals and live largely "in the moment." Parents and therapists in the field are doggedly focused on correcting behaviors after they occur, analyzing those behaviors with the child and helping them reflect on it, recall it, etc; all of this occurring post-behavior.

But I argue that if we're already analyzing behaviors, then an understanding of their causes lead to the conclusion that the behavior can be prevented by preventing the cause. The only drawback to this is that application is best accomplished with direct interaction; it is not readily applicable in an outpatient or weekly session type of setting without significant duration. This is because in order for Preemptive Behavior Therapy to work, you must be able to consistently and for sustained periods interact with and observe the child in question.

Consider a small puppy, at home with his new human family for the first time. Even inexperienced dog owners will quickly learn the puppy's body language. When the puppy loses interest in play for a moment, puts his nose to the ground and starts sniffing while trotting quickly in circles or back and forth, family members will suddenly jump up and take the dog outside, as they recognize the precursors that indicate an undesired behavior is about to occur.

Namely, the pooch is about to soil the carpet.

So then the family remains "on watch" and intervenes quickly when the puppy exhibits signs that it needs to urinate; a strong action plan but not one that is overly learning-enhanced for the animal in question.

Instead, a smart family takes this one step further and prevents any chance of bad behavior by taking the puppy outside immediately after it has slept, eaten, etc; the times when a puppy is most likely to relieve itself. Eventually the puppy learns to self-correct by "asking" to be let out, scratching at the door, using a pet door or otherwise doing its business in an appropriate way and in advance of the behavior event.

Preemptive Behavior Therapy is training at this basic pre-conscious, conditioned level. Skillful use of PBT requires excellent observation skills, knowledge and interpretation of body language, and the ability to redirect behaviors in as low-impact a manner as possible. We're not training to *correct* behaviors; we are learning how to *prevent* them from occurring by interrupting negative thought patterns and behavioral precursors. This is accomplished via a process of Redirections.

The PBT model uses social hierarchy and body language concepts based on observations of and interactions with horses and dogs, and in the coming chapters I'll relate some specific examples of stories where animal behavior has helped to shape the principles of PBT.

Moreover, the PBT model is especially useful in guiding troubled youth in self-corrective behaviors, and in fact was derived a great deal from my personal success in the field while working with at-risk kids. The goal of this type of therapy is to help kids and young people recognize and refuse the types of thinking and behaviors that lead to negative actions and subsequently, negative consequences. This book is for parents, teachers, clinicians, technicians and anyone else who holds significant responsibility for the welfare and progress of our youth. But most of all, this book is for our children.

1 FOUNDATIONS

The principles of Preemptive Behavior Therapy were born before I was. My mother rode horses while she was pregnant with me, which meant that I experienced the connection between man and horse while still in the womb.

So it was no surprise that I began riding before I was two years old – at first on a little pony named Obie. I had many adventures with Obie and learned a lot about animal behavior as we grew up together. Without recognizing it at the time, I learned how to "speak horse." We had other horses on the property where I grew up and I mimicked their body language; studying their nips, kicks, ear-flips and whinnies. I understood their language and did my human best to speak to our horses - especially Obie - in their language.

But I also discovered that horses can learn our language and physical expressions, and that real communication between a horse and a person is possible.

Soon I found out that this held true for many animals on our little farm; pigs, dogs, cats and chickens could all be communicated with if you knew how, and if you cared enough to try. While I was discovering this there was a quiet movement building elsewhere that I didn't yet know that I wanted to be a part of: the world of the Animal Communicator.

Even at a young age I seemed destined to spend my life working with animals. By the time I was 5 years old I had spent so many hours in the saddle that I won my first show-jumping event on a little pony we called

Dandy Mick. At age 6 I was riding harness on our family farm - causing my poor mother a great deal of worry as my rig raced across the landscape.

My childhood also raced by and I hardly noticed. I was completely absorbed with our animals and spent all of my time with them whenever I could. I would stand there and watch the horses and ponies chomp down their grain and hay in the mornings and pretend like I was one of them. I watched them speak to each other and their language was clear to me.

In fact, before my tenth birthday I had a stunning realization that animal communication was far more forthright and honest than human communication. I eventually learned when a horse was telling me that it was reluctant to go on because its frogs were sore, or that its stomach was upset. I learned when a horse, dog or pony wanted affection and when it wanted to be left alone.

But with people, I wasn't always certain. Humans often say one thing but mean another even when they don't intend to. Or they may say one thing with their words, but something entirely different with their body language.

With animals, there was never any question.

I thought about animal communication often, although I never really called it that. Sometimes I'd lie on my back and chew a piece of fresh hay while I listened to the horses graze. I'd stare up at the sky and watch clouds whip by, wondering how weird other people thought I was for constantly wanting to be around animals. I'd think that if I could just speak to other people as clearly as animals spoke to me, then I might have a chance of doing something great in life.

I didn't know exactly how I would do it, but I figured out early on that I simply *had* to work with animals - especially horses - and assumed that this would be my straight and narrow career path. But as it turned out, life had other things in store for me.

As I grew older my passion for all things equestrian deepened, expanded and matured. I was blessed with the opportunity to learn from some of Australia's best handlers, riders and trainers. Sometimes I played hard; covered in sweat, blood and dirt. Other times I worked hard even though it didn't seem like work at all. Eventually I became good enough to get comfortable with my life and love of horses, but I had other great loves as well.

One of these loves – the love of the complexity of human thought and emotion – beckoned me away from the arena and the paddocks and instead led me on an intense pursuit of the greater questions in life.

FROM HORSES TO HUMANS

I left the dusty fields and the babbling creeks I had come to know as a child and went off to study Philosophy at the Australian National University. Once there I found myself immersed in a completely new way of thinking; instead of pondering the immediacy of a horse's ears or the whites of their eyes, I pondered the limitless possibilities of an infinite universe. It was during this time that I began to learn that it was possible to create my own reality.

But reality is hard and philosophy is often no comfort. Some people chided me, saying that philosophy offered little substance for study. However, the more I searched, the more I questioned and sought, the more I came to believe that philosophy is the very study of substance itself!

I roamed about in my mind and in books, and ultimately it was these philosophical wanderings that led me to re-discover and ponder the reality of animal communication. There was a tide that pulled within me, calling me toward an anvil where I could smelt my love of horses with my love of philosophy. But I was young and I was torn in many directions, and so I became swept up in the current of life.

By some great blessing of the universe I was invited to earn my Doctorate of Philosophy in the U.S.A. by a visiting lecturer at ANU. I remember at the time marveling at the richness of this opportunity. I spent hours daydreaming about achieving my doctorate and the many ways I might be able to use my education to help other people. But while it might have seemed like the most logical path at the time, I chose another.

Instead of pursuing my doctorate, I became the Entertainment Manager for the Billabong hotel group in 1985. On the surface it seemed a strange choice, but it was actually one that suited me well. As I saw it, the foundation of entertainment was creation, and creation was only bound by inspiration. My training in philosophy served me dutifully in this regard, for I found inspiration everywhere in life and used this to ply my trade.

Although I was not conscious of it at the time, by my early adulthood I had learned to interpret human behavior based on my direct experience with animals. But this had been merged with my developing understanding of the human mind, and I found great success in the industry by listening for deeper types of communication. I often acted upon what I heard or sensed before clients and associates could articulate what they needed.

Part of my journey was that I wanted - needed - to help others. I don't know where this drive came from and I'm not sure whether it's because I never felt worthy or because I felt too much worth. What I do know is that I spent the next 15 years in the entertainment industry; working in various sectors in different areas of the country, and I thoroughly enjoyed all of it. However, as always I was pulled in many directions and my heart led the way.

You see, I found a thrill in helping my clients arrange concert venues or elaborate banquets, but there was a part of me that felt like these were hollow actions. The philosophical side of me could not shake a growing notion that I was helping those who needed nothing.

THE HOME FOR DYING DESTITUTES

We all have our heroes, and mine had been Mother Teresa since I was a little girl. Her benevolence, her steadfastness and her passion for humanity were traits that I had always hoped to develop in me. I studied her work and found so much beauty in it that I sent her a letter. I wanted to gush with adoration for her, but I somehow remained reserved when I praised her work and asked how I too might be of service.

I mailed that letter and thought nothing more of it. Life went on. Fans often write to their idols that are too busy being idolized to respond.

But not Mother Teresa.

Despite everything that she was doing for her fellow man at the time, she actually read my letter and responded by hand. Her response was short and graceful. She encouraged me to come to India to work with people who truly needed help, so I quit everything I was doing and left it all behind.

In 1987 I found myself in Calcutta at the Nirmal Hriday home for dying destitutes in Kalighat, Calcutta, India. I'll never forget how completely overwhelmed I felt as I stood in the dirt street looking at the door of the old temple. My throat clenched tight and my legs went numb as I approached the crumbling stairs. There were only 4 or 5 steps and they were well rounded with age, but they still managed to tower over me. I was scared, but I didn't know why. The philosophical voice inside of me was silent - quelled by an emotion older than humanity itself. I hesitated there at the bottom of the stairs for an agonizing eternity until I felt a powerful presence behind me.

A priest had approached while I fought my silent battle on those ancient steps. He was an enormous man with a towering voice and of towering height, but his smile was warm and disarming. He somehow knew it was my first time there and he reassured me gently; more with his smile and his eyes than with words. What he said instantly eroded the barrier between me and the threshold to Nirmal Hriday:

"Do not be fearful, child," he said, *"I know that in your country there is fear of death. Death is frightening for people to witness. But here, death is a solution. So there is no fear."*

And with those words I began my work alongside the Sisters at the home for dying destitutes. The place was also called the Home of the Pure Heart, and in my time there I saw that this was a much more fitting name.

Outsiders saw the home as a place of death and assumed sorrowful things happened within. But this couldn't have been further from the truth. The Home of the Pure Heart was about life, and though there was hardly any furniture and we operated at times with nothing but hope, I saw more of the best part of humanity in my time there than I ever had before or since.

What I learned at Nirmal Hriday shaped who I have become today. The Sisters helped me morph from a person who merely believed abstractly that there were "better ways," to a person committed to actually finding a better way.

Essentially, I learned that belief must be coupled with action in order to have real meaning. And that is when my life changed again. I left Calcutta and returned home, determined to find my way back to horses, fresh earth and a bit of the past.

RETREAT TO MOVE FORWARD

I went back to my roots and took up the reins again. I did some training here and there, but mostly I drove a carriage in Melbourne as my full-time gig. It seemed by the late 1990's I had come full-circle and was back in the saddle, so-to-speak.

I was buying time, in a way. After my work at Nirmal Hriday I knew that I wanted to do something that combined my love of horses with my love of people, and the first way I thought I might be able to do that was by driving a rig. However, it wasn't long before I tired of the tourists and realized that once again, I was primarily helping those who needed nothing.

But just when I thought I was on the wrong path, something began to happen. As I guided my carriage down Melbourne's streets, I started becoming familiar with the people who lived there; and I don't mean the ones who lived in the neatly lined houses and apartments. I'm talking about the actual street people; those who camped out in doorways and alleys; those who roamed from place to place with nowhere to settle, and those who otherwise lived on the fringes of society.

I'd pass these people every day and give a mighty "Whoa!" and bring my horses up to chat with them. We'd talk a bit and I became friendly with them. Some were old and could barely get around, some were alone, others in pairs or small groups. I developed a routine and with it I became a part of the neighborhoods and streets I traveled every day.

Despite the tattered rags for clothing and the crooked or missing teeth, despite the severe lack of traditional substance in their lives; a job, a home, family, resources, money, etc; despite this, not one of them ever tried to take advantage of me. And in the early days, they could have easily done so as I was rather naive.

But I learned quickly that poverty does not make anyone dangerous; it actually drains all of the fight right out of a person. I could see this in the eyes of the street people, and they could see that I knew. I was on the street every day; I was virtually one of them. My horse's hooves pounded the pavement from sunrise until sundown. The horses were one of them as well.

In this regard we were all unspoken family, and we watched out for each other.

When an old man who always stopped to pet the horses was shivering in a doorway one day, I brought him an old jacket from my carriage. When I was robbed at knifepoint, several street people came to my aid. We did what we could for each other, but I wanted to do more.

These were truly vulnerable and disadvantaged people. These were not drunken and spiteful bums, choosing to waste resources and charity on selfish things. These were the downtrodden and weary; these were people who had nothing. But surprisingly, they wanted nothing; only respect, and this I held in deep sincerity for many of them.

I met many people on the fringes of society during this time, and I have often spoken of them as "The Invisible People" or "The Forgotten People." Though most often I referred to them simply as my friends. But eventually the day came where I chose a new path, and I surrendered my reins so that my hands were free to reach out to whatever would come next.

A TROUBLED HORSE

A teacher can be anyone, or anything. It can be a parent or an enemy, a bird or a donkey, a book or a sunrise. In my case, it was a horse.

My time as a carriage driver on the streets of Melbourne was coming to an end when a teacher suddenly came into my life unannounced. His name was Cheung, and he set off a chain of events that would lead me deep into the world of animal communication.

Cheung was a magnificent Thoroughbred that had been severely traumatized and abused in the past. He was so filled with anxiety and terror that I would sometimes cry quietly while I watched him weave in the paddock with the whites of his eyes flashing. He was frightened of everything and reacted dangerously to even the most benign of events and interactions.

Cheung's fear reaction was so great that it seemed a safe working relationship with him would be impossible. I stayed near him for hours on end, day after day, just quietly standing there. I saw little progress but I kept at it.

For a while it seemed that there wasn't much hope for Cheung. He was too dangerous to walk – not because he was aggressive but because he didn't – no, *couldn't* - see me because he was too focused on his own fears. I'd try to lead him through the gate and he'd spook at the wind, eyes flashing, and then he'd bolt and practically barrel me over. I escaped injury on several occasions only by sheer luck.

Nevertheless, I went to see him every day. I talked to him, cooed to him, and sometimes we just sat quietly together. I waited every day for some sign of recognition; some spark of trust. But day after day there was nothing.

Eventually things got to the point where I started thinking the worst. It seemed like the only humane thing to do for this poor tortured soul would be to euthanize him.

But one day while Cheung was weaving crazily in his paddock I did something unexpected; I clapped my hands sharply and he suddenly stopped weaving and looked directly at me. It occurred to me in that moment that if I could redirect his attention consistently that I could get him to focus on trusting me. It was out of this event that my "Flicker" theory was born, which gradually developed into a technique for use with traumatized and vulnerable people and animals.

The basic principle of the Flicker method is to create a distraction or break in the undesirable behavior process and use this moment to redirect or refocus the animal using carefully calculated stimuli.

I honed this practice with Cheung using various distraction methods; clapping, using a clicker, a whistle, etc. Interestingly, it wasn't the type of distraction that mattered - Cheung's undesirable behavior could be momentarily arrested using many different tools - it was what happened when his attention was focused on me for that split second after the distraction that really mattered.

When the distraction occurs, it's relatively easy to train an animal to respond with newly focused attention. If I clapped my hands and Cheung stopped weaving, but then no further stimuli were presented, he'd quickly go back to being mental. If I repeated this a few times, eventually he'd learn that my hand clapping meant nothing.

But if I presented negative stimuli, then Cheung would quickly associate my clapping with dread. Conversely, rewarding the equine with a tasty treat would create a positive association, and clapping would soon be a favorite part of his day.

These are basic principles of training and the particular type of animal doesn't always matter; dogs, horses, pigs and other animals can be trained this way. But when it comes to traumatized animals, traditional training methods don't always work. You must first interrupt the negative behavior in order to re-train it out of the animal, and this requires the flicker method.

The primary concern with stressed or abused animals is that the redirection - the "flicker" - must be completely inert and neutral, and must be immediately followed with positive direction and reinforcement, or gentle "pressure," which I'll discuss later in this book.

Though discovered completely by accident, it was obvious to me from the beginning that here was something that just might work, and 'lo and behold, it did! Cheung began to come around. A sniff of my hand here, a small command obeyed there, and soon enough, he began to trust me and I him.

It took a massive amount of effort, but it wasn't long before I raced Cheung at an Amateur Day event that changed me forever. The way that magnificent animal moved underneath me that day was unlike anything I'd experienced before: whereas the pounding of the other horse's hooves were deafeningly frenetic, Cheung seemed to scarcely skim the surface of the warm earth before gliding off the front in an effortless display of raw power. He was smooth, beautiful and confident; so much so that it was almost impossible to imagine how he had once been.

He went from defeated to champion in just a short year, and I loved him.

A PUSH IN THE RIGHT DIRECTION

My biggest weakness is doubt. Not necessarily doubt itself, but my reaction to it. In the face of even the slightest doubt I sometimes balk unreasonably. Because I had no clear direction and wasn't sure that I could make it a success, I only worked the Flicker method among my local circles, and only when called upon. Doubt was dogging me.

But after word of my success with Cheung spread locally, I started getting phone calls, emails and letters from people who wanted me to work with their troubled horse or dog. I took on several cases and had great success, but I still doubted my own abilities and so never did anything to take Flicker to the next level. I knew that I needed just one thing in order to do this; to become a better communicator.

I needed to learn how to communicate better with animals, and I needed to learn how to communicate with myself and with other people. I knew this but I procrastinated because I didn't know how to get started.

Thankfully, the universe gave me a push in the right direction in the form of an old veterinarian friend of mine. After witnessing the results of my Flicker theory applied to Cheung, whom he knew well, he said;

"Get some business cards printed. There's work to be done."

In that moment, my life changed forever. The Seeker in me – the philosopher I had always been inside - suddenly rose up and proclaimed;

"Yes! If I can think it, it can be done!"

And from that moment forward my quest to become an animal communicator consumed me. Somewhere deep inside, I knew that I would one day be able to reach people through my ability to reach animals - it was just a matter of bridging that imaginary but stubborn gap.

I wasted no time and no expense. I flew across the Pacific to the United States and sought out Lydia Hiby; a pioneer in animal communication. Lydia was successful in communicating with Cheung, my troubled horse, in an event that moved me to the core of my being.

While communicating with my horse Lydia accurately described things she couldn't possibly have known. She talked about the race where Cheung floated across the sand. She described our home and Cheung's paddock. She knew about past trauma and injuries he had sustained.

At one point Lydia described how Cheung had been upset by my dog, Voss, who apparently had crept into Cheung's paddock while I was away. While she related this story I looked over at Voss (he was always nearby) and he quickly dropped his head and slunk off toward his bed, seemingly guilty-as-charged.

When I saw Lydia at work, I knew she was authentic. It was possible to physically feel the connection she had during an animal communication session; you could sense it even with your eyes closed and your ears plugged, because most of this communication is not vocalized in the traditional sense. Her passion and gift for speaking with those who had no voice inspired me and fueled me onward to become even more involved in this field.

Over the next few years my entire life was dedicated to animal communication. Lydia came to Australia in 2001 and we worked on this more, then in 2003 I travelled back to the U.S. to complete a workshop with her. During my time there I read a great deal about John Lyons; a man widely considered America's most trusted horseman. I knew that developing a comprehensive understanding of his work was the next step for me.

I decided to study under Ed Thornton in California – the only triple-certified John Lyons Conditioned Response Trainer in the world. I began an apprenticeship with him in 2005, and by 2006 I had qualified as a trainer. I finally felt like I understood enough about equine body language and vocalizations that I could start my work in earnest.

PURSUING DREAMS ONE AT A TIME

I felt it was time to put my newly acquired skills to use and pursue a childhood dream at the same time. As a young girl I had always wanted a true Mustang, and that dream came true for me when a dear friend connected me with a Mustang that was found in a pen in Nevada, U.S. I eventually took this horse, "Whisper", back to Australia with me and began working with her, and it was during this time that I discovered the work of Carol Gurney.

Carol, like Lydia Hiby, is a pioneer in the animal communication field. She is the founder of the Gurney Institute of Animal Communication – the most comprehensive certification program in the world. I knew that I could learn a lot from Carol, so I began my studies with her in 2009.

During this time other dreams started to fall into place naturally, and this included my work with disadvantaged and/or high-risk youth. Without quite realizing it at first, I began applying principles learned in the ring with horses in my daily functions as a youth protectorate and counselor.

There were too many similarities to ignore. I began to understand body language and its implications better, and I found that I could interrupt negative behaviors with an adaptive form of the Flicker. I didn't experiment with this deliberately or openly, instead this was a natural evolution of things based on what worked and what felt right.

Eventually I began to philosophize about the Flicker method in order to flesh it out more fully as a concept, and it was then that I realized that Flicker was merely a stepping stone to correct a negative behavior once it was already occurring. But what if the negative behavior could be prevented altogether?

This is when Preemptive Behavior Therapy was born. I learned through hard experience that body language and other signs can give us clues about what a person (or horse) is feeling, and what they are most likely to do next.

By careful observation we can take action to redirect a behavior before it ever occurs, resulting in a passive type of correction. This correction also acts as a secondary training mechanism that over time will condition a person or animal to correct their own behaviors and bring their emotions under control and into perspective without negativity; and most of the time without prompting.

The beauty of PBT is that, ideally, there is no punishment involved. In most cases corrections are actually nothing more than redirections, although in some instances more direct action may be required. In order to apply these principles you must first retrain yourself in a number of ways, including taking a look at what your own body language is telling other people, and giving up on the traditional types of corrections and punishments meted out by most modern societies.

I find it fascinating, how life works – how we get from one place to the next. I remember when a professor at Melbourne University asked me at age 20 to give a series of lectures how I had stood in frozen terror at the lectern until I finally, fumblingly started to talk.

Today, I am a storyteller and I am passionate about public speaking and it comes easily for me.

Years ago, I could not clear my thoughts long enough to pen a letter, never mind a book. Today I have a message that I know is worth sharing, and the journey that got me this far is only part of that story. But I'm proud to share it with you, and I hope it helps to understand where these ideas came from and how they developed.

2 WHY THE OLD WAYS ARE DYING

It wasn't long ago that whipping a child was considered a perfectly acceptable form of punishment. In fact, even today corporal punishment is still used in many parts of the world. But overall humans seem to be moving toward less aggressive and certainly less violent methods of parenting and teaching.

As the world shrinks due to the elimination of borders thanks to the internet and other media channels, there has been a surge of parenting and teaching models that have been developed and/or renewed in the last 2 decades. However, despite the fact that, to my knowledge, the principles of Preemptive Behavior Therapy are not deliberately being practiced in any homes or institutions, I still believe it is a very old teaching model.

We know for example that early martial artists studied and mimicked animals with much success. (1) We also know that many indigenous peoples in Australia, the Americas and Africa held animals in high regard and were intimately familiar with their body language and vocalizations. In fact, some of these peoples dressed like the animals they hunted and tracked in the earliest displays I can think of showing humans deliberately trying to understand the creatures around them.

So when I say that the old ways are dying, that's only partially true. PBT is actually based on an ancient observation and teaching model that evolved naturally before the invention of writing. I believe that early peoples must have taught their children and interacted with them based at least partly on their observations of how other mammals interacted with their offspring.

Today we are so far removed from this type of living that the entire concept of raising a child based largely on observations made in the animal world seems far-fetched. But is it? Are we not animals, mammals, instinctual creatures? We are, and PBT works for precisely this reason.

If you try to imagine yourself as an outsider to the human race for a moment, you'll find that observing humans for just a short amount of time is extremely fascinating. This is because when you watch other humans in this capacity, the behavior that you see generally defies language and culture.

Body language is largely universal because we are all instinctual humans responding physically to our environment. These response mechanisms are ancient and deeply ingrained in us, and most of the time these physical responses are occurring without our conscious knowledge.

But when you begin to look at body language as an outsider, it's clear that humans communicate a great deal with their bodies. The problem is that we're listening to these cues whether we are aware of it or not, and this body language often conflicts with what a person is actually saying verbally. This results in communication challenges that most of us are all too familiar with.

Unfortunately, we've come to a crossroads in our ultra-modern post-progressive societies. The teaching of our children is being carried out in under-qualified, poorly funded schools by teachers who are overwhelmed and underpaid. The rearing of the main body of our children is difficult enough, but when troubled, traumatized or otherwise damaged youth are in question, it seems like they're the ones most often thrown under the bus.

The solution chosen in many cases is to segregate these children by putting them in special classes, special schools, special homes or institutions. Then it's up to people like me and those I work with to help try to put the pieces back together and ensure that these children and young adults get what they need in order to overcome their challenges and become a productive member of society. With the tools that we are given, this is generally a bleak task.

But at least none of us are alone. This is some comfort despite the fact that parents and teachers face the same battles every day, and it appears that things are not going well based on the most common methods of managing at-risk kids:

*Punishment

Punishment seems like a natural part of parenting, and with so many different ways to punish a child today, it's an easy choice to correct undesirable behaviors. Unfortunately, many parents, teachers and clinicians don't know how to punish correctly, and most don't understand that there are better ways to prevent negative behavior than via direct punishments. After all, if you directly punish a child for every negative infraction, the effectiveness of the punishment is reduced through something akin to immunity. After this point, the only option is more and more severe punishments.

*Medication

Our children are over-medicated. We treat most behavioral problems like they are genuine clinical disorders worthy of treatment with potent chemicals like Zoloft, Paxil, Seroquel and others. There seems to be a diagnosis for nearly every child and a corresponding group of medications to go along with these diagnoses.

I attribute most of this cultural failure to the fact that medication is the easy way out. We've become lazy societies and a pill is the simplest and fastest solution to everything from weight loss to an unruly child. For thousands of years parents and educators have fought the same wars with youth that we battle today, but it's only recently that we've sought to control these obviously natural and normal tendencies with chemicals.

It's easier that way. Or at least, that's what it seems like when a doctor says that a couple of pills each day will solve any pesky behavioral problems. It's just too easy.

There are those who have proclaimed - some of them loudly - that these types of medications and others like them are responsible for the sudden spate of killings in US schools over the past quarter century. I am inclined to believe this, although in my experience the data to support this is not easy to come by.

Of course, there are legitimate cases where medication is the right choice, but I think that this is the exception rather than the rule. I firmly believe that in most cases medication is not necessary; instead, the right teaching model is all that is lacking.

*Hospitalization - The amount of children placed in hospitals or other institutions worldwide as a result of behavioral problems is astonishing, and records probably do not reflect anything close to the actual numbers. Of course, in most instances medication is the preferred course of treatment for problematic children and youth, which brings us back to my segment on medications above. In my opinion, hospitalization should only be used as a temporary, last-resort measure to protect a child from himself or others.

*Segregation - It often starts in grade school or high school - children who have behavioral issues, outbursts or difficulties getting along with peers are often segregated. This can be something as simple as detention, but it often escalates to special classes and "alternative" programs that do little more than group such kids together and keep them out of everyone's way.

Segregation is extremely damaging to a child's psychological development, not to mention the fact that it's unhealthy for humans to be segregated against their will. We are highly social creatures and interaction with others is a vital health function. Use this primitive need as a type of punishment, and the results will probably not be what you're expecting.

For example, consider a small puppy; Spot. Spot is just one of 8 puppies in a litter, and he's having a really rough time learning to go potty outside. He has continual accidents and eventually the owner separates the animal from its litter mates as a "solution" in order to administer a different type of training for the pup.

However, this separation is far more severe than the behavior in question and therefore is little more than a cruel punishment. The puppy will yearn to get back to its mates and may eventually suffer psychological damage if he is withheld from them long enough. This type of isolation/separation is not conducive to a good learning environment.

Children are just as highly social as puppies and have complex hierarchies among them. If we expect troubled youth to function normally in society, but then we teach them early on that they're so different and undesirable that they must be segregated, then we're really doing them a disservice and setting them up for failure.

*Intervention

Interventions are a common method of dealing with at risk youth, but I believe they are also one of the most damaging when conducted improperly. The problem is that interventions are often highly confrontational and are launched as a surprise as a matter of course. In case after case, the subject of the intervention feels attacked and so naturally and instinctually counters with an offensive or defensive position, thereby generating the very behavior that the intervention sought to address in the first place.

I often feel the same way about interventions as I do about medication - it's an easier way out. Instead of doing the hard work required to teach a child the correct way, it's easier to pass the buck in the form of a pill, or an expert and some friends and family in the form of a surprise intervention.

Let's say you've got a horse that likes to harass and nip at the other horses in his paddock. If you segregate him, it will hurt him psychologically. If you medicate him, he'll be a useless mess. If you suddenly and without warning stick him in a room full of the horses and handlers he's been in trouble with, and you permit those horses and handlers to complain about the horse, you can bet there's going to be a fight. In fact, you'd never even get the horse in that room at all; he'd balk on the way in and run like hell.

In reality, a troubled child is the same as an unruly stallion. Confrontational solutions are just not wise, and there's almost no way that a surprise intervention will be seen as anything but a confrontation and a "ganging up" on the target of the intervention.

*Restraint

You can physically prevent a child from engaging in harmful or negative behavior. You can lock them in a room, cut off their communication privileges, segregate them, medicate them or hospitalize them, but you're not teaching them anything except that you can't be trusted.

Restraint is essentially the same thing that we do to prisoners; we house them in a secure location where they cannot get into trouble with the public. But what do we teach them? Where is the rehabilitation in this? Prison amounts to nothing less than warehousing an individual, which means that when they are released, they have not changed except that they have probably become more hardened.

The same is true of restraint. If a child is engaging in a negative behavior such as sneaking out at night, and your solution is to install locks on the windows and doors, how have you taught the child anything? What you taught them is that there is a way around their behaviors - an easy way out - and this tells them by default that there is also a way around your restraints, and the cycle goes on.

If you take this same child and segregate them by moving away from the area in order to remove the motivation to sneak out, all you're doing is buying time until that motivation is found again once things have settled down. You haven't taught the child anything except that there are consequences for actions. But we all already know this, and we know it from a very early age.

These methods of managing and correcting at-risk children are the same methods being used with kids from nearly all demographics, and they are all part of the 4 main types of parenting. Parenting is essentially what we do in our roles as social workers, educators, clinicians, counselors and of course as parents. We all also fall into one or more of the following roles while in these positions:

*Authoritative

Authoritative: "having the confident quality of someone who is respected or obeyed by other people" "clearly accurate or knowledgeable" -From the Merriam-Webster Online Dictionary

The Authoritative style of parenting is a well-balanced method of child rearing that operates primarily through intellect. First developed as a concept by Diana Baumrind, this parenting style is often lauded as the most likely to result in successful, well-adjusted offspring.

"[authoritative parents] monitor and impart clear standards for their children's conduct. They are assertive, but not intrusive and restrictive. Their disciplinary methods are supportive, rather than punitive. They want their children to be assertive as well as socially responsible, and self-regulated as well as cooperative" (Baumrind, 1991, p. 62).

*Authoritarian

Authoritarian: expecting or requiring people to obey rules or laws: not allowing personal freedom -From the Merriam-Webster Online Dictionary

This type of parenting is exceptionally strict and is neither intellectually based nor emotionally based. Instead, the principle focus is on rule setting and enforcement.

"[these types of parents] are obedience- and status-oriented, and expect their orders to be obeyed without explanation" (Baumrind, 1991, p. 62)

*Indulgent/Permissive

Indulgent parents are more friendly than authoritative, allowing their children to largely do as they want with few restrictions and virtually no punishment. They are emotionally available to their children but demand very little from them.

"[permissive parents] are more responsive than they are demanding. They are nontraditional and lenient, do not require mature behavior, allow considerable self-regulation, and avoid confrontation" (Baumrind 1991)

*Neglectful/Uninvolved

According to Maccoby and Martin (1983), Neglectful parents are those who provide basic needs only. They are not emotionally or intellectually available to their children and they communicate infrequently, however, they are not abusive.

*Attachment

Attachment parenting is a subset parenting style as originally described by Pediatrician William Sears and theorized by John Bowlby. This type of parenting focuses primarily on strengthening the bond between parent/caregiver and child. This bond is foundationally emotional and can be as focused on the parent as it is on the child.

ALL TYPES OF PARENTING MAY BE EQUALLY EFFECTIVE

Noted sociologist Frank Furedi argued that parenting styles aren't nearly as important as widely believed and that children can develop well in just about any type of environment that isn't abusive or neglectful. Author and scholar Judith Rich Harris echoed this sentiment, arguing that parenting styles do not have a significant effect on developmental outcomes for children short of traumatic upbringing.

Although these parenting styles offer significant opportunity for success in child rearing (although perhaps as noted above only through default), not one of them addresses instinctual behavioral cues as a modus operandi.

This means that Preemptive Behavior Therapy can bolster and strengthen all parenting types and styles. It doesn't matter whether a person uses one or more of these styles - they can all benefit from PBT because they all have the same ultimate goal; well-behaved, emotionally-stable children that can self-regulate their behavior.

What we need to understand is that children (and adults) exhibit animalistic traits that we can learn to recognize in advance of negative behavior and subsequently take appropriate action to correct or redirect the behavior before it occurs. This largely "preempts" the need for any particular parenting style; by focusing on preempting the behavior, we eliminate the need for punishment and teach self-correction at a very early age. Ultimately, this leaves more time to build trust and develop emotional bonds.

Unfortunately, changing attitudes about parenting are causing the focus to shift from what works to what is popular, and social media and our electronic interconnectivity is sometimes causing more harm than good in this regard. We see this clearly displayed in our faulty sets of priorities as indicated by modern social chatter and sharing; our cultural priorities have shifted and resulted in some bad behavior and traits among both children and adults:

*Sense of Entitlement
*Fear of Discipline
*Poor ambition
*Lack of Values

THE EVIDENCE IS ALL AROUND US

How do we know these old ways are not working? How do we know that even the "best" parenting style needs something more? Just open the paper. Read the news online. Talk to kids at school.

Nearly every day there's a new shooting, a new stabbing or a new suicide. Bullying is rampant and parents take very little responsibility for their children. We've got children who are overweight, overmedicated and oversexed being led by parents and other authority figures who share the same traits. We've got a youth prison system, youth court system, and plenty of secure concrete and steel locations to coldly house misbehaving children.

We have insanely popular television shows that glamorize teen pregnancy. Our children's most prominent role models are selfish, largely talentless and badly behaved stars and starlets that perpetuate some of the most awful behaviors occurring in kids today.

We've got kids being kicked out of school for praying, and other kids being kicked out for standing up to bullies. We've got bullies that are supported by demented teachers. We've got 3rd graders bringing guns to school and entire television shows that celebrate ignorance and sloth. We've got grade school kids having sex and rumors of candied drugs circulating in our schools.

Our streets are overrun by youth gangs and youth centers, youth shelters and soup kitchens. We've got well-off parents in suburbia medicating their depressed kids with drugs that are thought to cause suicidal ideations.

Everywhere you look there are appalling messages being blasted at our kids and young people; there is no reprieve and nowhere to hide from it all. From social media to radio to visual and audio ads at the end of every aisle in every store, we're constantly slinging smut and bad behavior, and then we want an easy and fast solution when we don't like the results.

I say "we" because we are all at fault. This is my responsibility, and it is yours too.

How did we get here? We grew up too fast, and technology has mired us in confusion. Today many parents either discipline their kids too much and too sharply, or they don't discipline them at all. Many parents are afraid to punish or correct their children because of the potential for damaging consequences.

We're glued to one square after another; from computer screens to our cell phones to the dashboards in our cars and to television we watch at home, we're becoming more and more technology-oriented each day, all the while forgetting that we are physical creatures.

Today our children probably spend more time talking to people via social media and cell phones in an average day than they do talking to their parents. But the minute there's a problem, we all want a fast solution. From 5-minute rice to a 'script called in from a doctor that you just met, it's easy to take the easy way out.

We got to where we are today through laziness and complacency. But it doesn't have to be this way, and I believe the answers to these problems may be found in the Flicker method and Preemptive Behavior Therapy. And while these practices are primarily geared for troubled, traumatized and high risk children and adolescents, they can be applied in even the most loving and stable home with significant positive results.

We know that the old ways are not working because we see it all around us. The good news is that we are aware, and if you're reading this book, then you are one of the people who are about to set out to change things. Even if you only apply these principles with your children at home, your children will go out and leave their mark on the world, and it will be a better place for it.

But if you are a clinician, social worker, teacher or other person who works with troubled kids, you're going to find that you can achieve the unthinkable. We've all had that child that we thought was beyond repair - the child who had been traumatized so badly that there was just no return from that dark world for them. We've all had our Cheung; we've all stood outside the fence and sobbed, wishing we could break the wall down with our heart, our hands or our minds. But if you look, you'll see a *Flicker*, and in that moment, you'll realize that even the most tightly shut door has a window around the back.

References:

(1) https://www.blackbeltmag.com/category/kung-fu-animals-traditional-martial-arts-training/

3 BODY LANGUAGE & THE FLICKER

We listen to very little of what people actually say. The most commonly referenced statistic in this regard is based on data developed by Dr. Albert Mehrabian, a noted author and expert on nonverbal communication. This statistic shows that only 7% of certain types of communication between humans are verbal. (1)

This is partly because many people are so distracted with their own thoughts that they cannot entirely pay attention to a conversation - even an important one. Instead, we gain more information and understand what is being conveyed through body language than through speech. This is true despite the fact that most people aren't even aware that they are both displaying body language and reading/interpreting it all the time.

Ultimately, the most important type of communication is nonverbal because it is the most authentic. Body language is mostly instinctual or evolutionary and is sometimes the result of biological processes. For instance, the widening of eyes during a fear-inducing event is likely tied to a fight-or-flight response; wider eyes permits more light to enter the eyes, improving vision and thereby theoretically increasing the chances of survival.

Another example is a pursed mouth or drawn lips, which famed body language expert Joe Navarro attributes to distaste for something, stemming from an evolutionary response to bad food or drink. In this case, the mouth physically retracts from potentially sickening food. (2)

Of course, some body language is almost certainly learned. A mother who taps her foot when nervous may pass this behavior on to her daughter. A father who avoids eye contact during stressful interactions may have a son who does the same.

To parents, teachers and clinicians body language is a two way street; we can use our understanding of nonverbal communication to decipher a child's true feelings or intent, but by the same token, we betray our true feelings with our own body language.

For instance, consider the clinician working in a home for troubled youth. Should the youth explode and launch an aggressive verbal tirade, the clinician must not show fear or anger. The problem is that we're human beings, and this is very difficult to do. We can lie with our words by saying that we're not upset, but our body language tells a different story.

From an evolutionary standpoint, body language identifies us as predator or prey in a natural environment. When teaching a child, we must appear as neither predator nor prey, and this is the most difficult balance that we can strike. This means that first and foremost, we must become aware of our own body language and quickly gain control over it. Then we must learn how to identify what body language means when exhibited by the young people that we work with.

However, it should be made clear that this is only the foundation of Preemptive Behavior Therapy. Once you learn to recognize nonverbal cues, you must be able to rapidly and accurately address them. This is where the Flicker theory comes in, and it can be stated thusly:

"Flicker is the practice of recognizing key nonverbal cues and creating a distraction or interruption in thinking during this critical moment in order to achieve a desired behavior or prevent an undesirable one."

The heart of PBT is what to do once you have interrupted the behavior, and how to use this process to develop a healthy and consistent cycle of self-correction.

To demonstrate how this is achieved, I'd like to discuss the body language of two animals that are familiar to most people. We'll imagine that these animals are in an extremely stressful situation, which is often the case for disadvantaged or troubled youth.

A Dog about to Attack: I've witnessed this numerous times in my life, and I think the experience is largely universal. A dog who is about to attack will have ears back or flattened (to protect in the event of a fight), lips bared and teeth exposed (to show the animal's primary weapon), hackles raised (to appear larger and more formidable), shoulders squared and lowered (to gain gravitational advantage) and eyes narrowed (to protect from injury).

A Horse about to Flee: I have been in the saddle when my horse suddenly spooked. Ahead on the trail something moved among the brush, and my horse froze (to avoid being seen by a predator), perked his ears up (to better hear the danger), widened his eyes (to take in more light and get a better visual on the threat), stood up taller, with shoulders wide and rear tight (ready to rapidly flee in a burst of speed) and started breathing more deeply and rapidly (to bring more oxygen-rich blood to muscles).

The responses that we see in dogs and horses are evolutionary, biological responses, and humans have them too. We call it body language, and for the most part we ignore it. But now try to imagine a child in similar situations as the dog and the horse above. Can you brainstorm based on experience what types of body language you might expect from a child about to flee? What about from a child about to have a violent outburst? Looking at it in this light, it's easy to see how what might appear as simple body language is in reality powerful physical responses to the environment around us.

These responses reveal far more about our state of mind than our words.

Nearly all of us can probably paint an accurate picture of what we might expect from a child about to fight or flee, and some may think that this is hardly news. But what about your own body language toward this child during these events - have you considered it honestly and thoroughly?

Chances are, probably not. And even for those that have, recognizing these nonverbal cues in ourselves and in the children we teach is one of the foundations of PBT, but there's much more work to be done once you recognize what's going on. The entire concept is to prevent the negative behavior from ever occurring by identifying early warning signs (nonverbal cues) and quickly redirecting them.

The following nonverbal cues are taken primarily from my direct experience in the field but are bolstered by experts as well:

1. HANDS

The hands are one of the most expressive communication tools that we have, capable of delivering a wide range of messages without our conscious direction. Of course, there are also a number of learned individuals who deliberately direct their hand movement during communication because they are aware of how this will affect the other person's ability to understand them.

Unless they have been raised in fundamentally bizarre circumstances, many at-risk and troubled kids will use their hands subconsciously to communicate, but you may have to "listen" harder. Years of trauma and abuse can render a child submissive and shy, afraid to use their hands when communicating. This is likely due to a desire to do nothing that will attract the attention of an abuser or other threat. In cases like this, it's important to watch what a child does with their hands, but it's just as important to observe what they **don't** do with their hands.

The following are some of the most common ways that hands are used to communicate or shut down communication. For the sake of this book, we'll stick to examples that are related to the field of high risk youth behavioral management.

Folded - folded hands often means that a child is paying attention or preparing to receive instruction. In my experience, hands that are folded with fingers interlaced indicate a higher degree of possible anxiety or readiness than hands that are folded on top of each other. The latter position often indicates deliberate reception mixed with repentance in some way. This position with one hand on top of a fist falls somewhere in the middle of these implied attitudes - willing reception mixed with some amount of angst or stress/pressure.

Tented - I have rarely seen this hand position in the young people that I have worked with. In my experience this is generally reserved for adults. However, there are 2 instances where I have seen children use this hand position:

1. Some highly intelligent children will tent their hands when they feel confident during an interaction, or when they are imparting some new information that the speaker isn't likely to know. In this case the fingertips are often pressed together, but the palms are spaced slightly apart. This indicates a receptive child, but one who is expecting to be heard and is eager to speak.

2. I have witnessed extremely stressed children tent their hands together when they feel that something bad is about to happen, or when they have just been told some bad news. It's almost as if these children were praying;

fingers and palms are both pressed tightly together in this case, and the hands are invariably held together in front of the chest. This indicates a protective stance where the child is subconsciously safeguarding against some type of perceived or actual danger.

Massaging - Nearly every time I have seen a child rub their hands, it is an indication of either shame or quiet confusion. I think this is a soothing type of body language as it allows the child to avoid eye contact in favor of physical fixation. This allows them time to think about their answers, and children are no fools - they know this makes them appear pensive, even if they can't articulate this effect.

The frequency and intensity of hand rubbing is indicative of how stressed the situation is making the child. The more rubbing occurs, the more stressful the situation is. (Navarro 2010) Because rubbing the hands produces heat and friction, hands that appear red and hot are likely indicators of extremely high stress considering that in most cases, stress pulls blood back to the internal organs, leaving the hands somewhat cold and hard. This is a result of our evolutionary flight-or-fight mechanism, which restricts blood flow to the extremities in order to give more power to the heart and lungs, thus enabling us to run faster and fight harder.

Clenched - When the hands are clenched, they're ready for a fight. This indicates a child who is angry, or one who is about to shut down. In most cases, there is a difference in the communication imparted from a clenched hand with the thumb on the outside, and with the thumb on the inside. In my experience in the field, the thumb on the inside does not indicate anxiety and anger. Instead, it's often a sign of fidgeting, and it usually doesn't last long. This is not a comfortable position for most people, whether they are experiencing stress or not.

Clenched hands with the thumb on the outside are the classical symbol of anger being kept in check, but only if the thumb is clenched against the hands. If the thumb is sticking out, indifference or even contentment is indicated.

As people who work with troubled kids, the clenched fist with thumb on the outside is one of the most pressing types of body language, as it tells us that we need to take action to defuse those fists. This can be accomplished a number of ways, but our primary point now is that this is a warning sign. Heed it.

Palms Up - I have seen many children plead with their palms up, but refute with their palms down. Any gestures made with the palms facing up are often quizzical in nature and seek reconciliation, solidarity or belief of some sort. This hand position is essentially saying "I am unarmed and defenseless. Please hear me or believe me."

Palms Down - This hand gesture is meant to refute, prevent, or protect from something, depending on the overall positioning of the hands and whether they are active or not. Active palms-down hands generally indicate aversion, while restful palms-down is indicative of indifference, restfulness or boredom.

However, palms-down rubbing - especially rubbing along the length of the legs - indicates nervousness and stress, and could be caused in part by the need to dry sweaty hands. In fact, I once knew of a teenager who rubbed his hands palm-down along his legs so much that he eventually wore long white streaks in all of his jeans. He was a very nervous individual, and the intensity of his hand-rubbing was directly and obviously related to how stressed or nervous he was at the moment.

Interlaced Rubbing - This isn't a common trait in young kids, but I have witnessed it many times with older children and teens. I have long since learned to recognize it as an indicator of stress, but former FBI counterintelligence officer Joe Navarro has stated that in his experience, this type of body language is usually reserved for admitting bad behavior. (3) I find his assessment to be accurate, as in most cases where I have seen these hand cues, it is in relation to a confession of some sort. This can be a confession of some specific act, a feeling, or an elaboration of other previously revealed ideas or concepts.

Sweeping Gestures - Sweeping gestures are tricky to decipher. In my experience, you must know the child for a little while before you will be able to determine what this type of body language means. Large gestures with the arms generally indicate excitement regarding the discussion or topic at hand. A child who sweeps their arms during an interaction may be trying to convey an idea that - to them - is large or complex. (4)

Other times these gestures may mean nothing at all. For instance, I have worked with many children who are extremely excitable. Some of them have legitimate, severe cases of conditions such as ADHD, which lends to this sort of gesticulation. However, children who are not normally considered hyperactive may suddenly use large hand gestures if something extremely exciting or important occurs.

Whatever the case may be, children who use these types of hand movements are trying to tell you something that is meaningful and timely.

Your response is critical, because the way that you respond to this type of body language will have an immediate impact on the behaviors that follow. Shutting down these large gestures may be a serious blow to a child. This is because when sweeping the arms widely, the child exposes their chest and neck, which can be interpreted as a signal of comfort with you or a particular situation. However, it can also signal displeasure, as if to say; *"look around at my environment and hear me out."*

Covering Face - Any good cop will tell you that a person who covers their face, neck or hair with their hands while talking are likely hiding something or outright lying. However, I'm not so sure about this, as it's also well-known that we touch our face something like 2000-5000 times each day. So either we all do a lot of lying in a day, or a lot of our face-touching is incidental and therefore we might not be lying as much as some authorities may think.

Nevertheless, I think that it is important to distinguish certain types of face touching that I have observed while working with high-risk youth. The most common hand gesture that I think generally indicates a problem is one or more hands covering the mouth. In many cases this is seemingly related to a child attempting to hold back something, and in my experience this is more often than not a victim experience being repressed in some way, and not a lie.

What I do find to indicate dishonesty is neck-rubbing. This is usually done with one hand and is a body cue I have seen most often in boys. For girls, fidgeting is more common.

When both hands are used to completely cover the mouth or face, this is often a sign of shame and may or may not be related to actual guilt.

Fidgeting - In the clinical or institutional setting, I associate fidgeting first and foremost with physical discomfort. This is especially true with children who are taking certain medications. Taking some step to alleviate this discomfort can go a long way toward building trust with the child.

In cases where fidgeting also may indicate emotional discomfort or stress, there are usually other signs associated with this that can be used to confirm the nature of the fidgeting. This includes poor eye contact, mumbling, and audible indications of frustration such as sighing, groaning and other signs of exasperation.

Natural or physical discomfort fidgeting involves constantly changing the entire general sitting or standing position. Stress-related fidgeting on the other hand is more focused - the hands seek out and consistently manipulate or tweak buttons, fasteners or other bits of clothing, or the hands may pick at imaginary bits of dirt. I have seen some highly intelligent children take up writing in notebooks during difficult conversations so as to keep their fidgeting obscured. I have also worked with kids who traced circles and other shapes on their legs, and one who admitted to spelling out the words of conversations in cursive with his index finger and thumb.

Biting Nails / Cracking Knuckles - Nail biting is often compared to fidgeting in children, and many children who exhibit this trait have some type of co-occurring condition such as ADHD, ODD, SAD or other disorders. (5) However, in their article *"Nail biting: Why it happens and what to do about it,"* authors Beth Haiken and Ann Bartz assert that in children, nail biting is primarily an unconscious behavior. (6)

Unfortunately, nail biting is not an easily explained behavior. Some children may do this simply out of boredom, while others may bite their nails excessively out of stress or frustration. When working with at risk youth, I find that nail biting is most common in girls and usually indicates that too much attention is being focused on the child. This could be a strong signal that redirection is required.

Knuckle cracking, on the other hand, is not something I have seen often. In most cases that I have witnessed, knuckle cracking is a habit learned from parents or caretakers, and may or may not be stress related.

In some cases children learn to recognize even the slightest buildup of pressure in their knuckles and seek to relieve this pressure, even though it causes no discomfort. In other cases I have received the distinct feeling that kids think knuckle cracking is cool, as the time that I most often see this behavior is in a group setting where other kids or adults are present that the child is seeking to impress. Take note of this.

Sitting on Hands - Despite popular belief, more often than not the kids that I have worked with have indicated comfort by sitting on their hands. I have spoken to other counselors, caseworkers, teachers and parents who all generally agree that a child who is sitting on their hands - especially during a conversation or interaction of some sort - is withholding information or trying to remain calm. But this is not my experience.

The way I see it, kids who have been abused or traumatized learn very quickly that their hands are not only a means of protection, but also a means of communicating when their voice might not work so well with the adults in their life. Kids that sit on their hands are comfortable enough to do so. After all, when in this position the hands are immobilized and the entire chest, neck and head are exposed. This is a vulnerable position for a child to be in; especially a high-risk or troubled child.

It's also important to account for the fact that some kids sit on their hands when they are cold.

No Hand Movement - No hand movement is, in my experience, the sign of a defeated child. Children are nearly always moving in some way whether they're aware of it or not, so I pay very close attention when I see a child who has shut down and is not moving their hands or arms at all. In nearly all instances where I have seen this, the child in question has also stopped speaking, or mostly so. At this stage communication becomes challenging because the child already feels that they cannot win. If you're seeing this type of body language, it's important to empower the child in some way without giving in to unreasonable demands.

Hand Presentation - You'd be surprised what you can learn by observing hand presentation. For instance, consider your first interaction with a child in an institutional setting. As you enter the room for the first time, you'll likely offer to shake the child's hand if they seem receptive enough. During this interaction, you can quickly assess many things:

Are the nails bitten down? Are there injuries that indicate physical confrontations, self-mutilation, or a child that is accident-prone? Are the hands sweaty and hot? Cold and clammy? Is the child fidgeting? Rubbing his or her neck or covering their mouth?

As you can see, you can gain a significant amount of useful information about a child within 1-3 seconds of your initial meeting with them. And all of this is just from the hands. Thankfully, there are many more types of body language and physical cues that can provide us with valuable information that we may not be able to obtain otherwise.

2. FEET & LEGS

Most people are unaware of their own body language and pay no conscious attention to the body language of others. However, even those people who study, catalogue and practice body language often stop short at the feet and legs. The majority of body language experts concentrate primarily on the hands, facial expressions and general body language of the torso, neck and shoulders. However, according to some of the world's most renowned experts on body language like Joe Navarro, James Borg and Edward T. Hall, the feet are often the most accurate predictor of true meaning, intention and honesty.

When it comes to the feet and legs, the direction these appendages point toward is indicative of interest. If the feet point directly at you during a conversation, you can probably assume that the child is interested and paying full attention to you. However, if the feet are pointing toward the exit of the room, this could indicate that the child is not interested and is indeed pointing out their true desire to leave the conversation by pointing their feet where they want to go.

This also applies to the knees; knees that are bent and pointing toward a particular person most likely means that the child is interested in that person. This could be a critical piece of information; especially in a group setting.

For instance, consider a situation where there has been some sort of confrontation or argument between several youth in a residential or institutional setting. If there are two children in particular that are accused of being aggressors in some way, watch the positioning of their knees and feet. If they're in cahoots, they'll likely be pointing at each other.

If the spat is between two children, it's easy to see which is ready for reconciliation and which is insistent on continuing the grudge simply by watching where their knees and feet point. If the general body language points away from you as the speaker and from the other child, you can be certain that the child in question is not interested in resolving the issue.

This is also an excellent indicator of romantic interest - something co-ed facilities would do well to heed. If there is a group of children in a room, look at the direction the feet and knees are pointing in to determine not only romantic interest, but also collusion and friendship between the kids.

We can also gain a great deal of information about the open or closed position of the legs and feet. Any athlete will tell you that superior performance requires the proper stance, and this generally takes the shape of feet and legs that are spaced apart in order to achieve a better state of balance and properly position the body to perform.

This can easily be translated to our field. Children who are receptive to your ideas will often have their legs and feet slightly open in addition to being pointed in your direction. Children who are closed to your ideas will likely close their body positioning to you by tightening their ankles, closing or crossing their legs, or pointing their knees away from you. These are important cues, even if the torso and head are still seemingly oriented toward you or another speaker in the room.

In addition to the fact that children will point to where they want to "go" with their feet, legs and knees, they also create some other important body language with their legs and feet that can tell you a great deal about their state of mind. Some of these are similar to physical cues put out by the hands. For instance, the legs can bounce up and down on the balls of the feet, the feet may kick the legs of a chair or other piece of furniture, or the legs may open and close nervously. These are often indicators of stress, anxiety, or uncertainty. However, it is your responsibility to interact with the child and learn from them enough to know when these signs are nothing more than the result of too much pent up physical energy or simply a way to pass the time.

3. NECK & SHOULDERS

It has always been surprising to me how much a child can tell you with his neck and shoulders. Unfortunately, I don't think this section is going to teach you much that most people don't already know, as this body language is nearly universal.

Overall, a straight neck and squared, open shoulders indicates receptivity and confidence. Slumped shoulders and bent neck indicates exhaustion, shame, depression or fear. In some cases I have seen children slump practically to the point of bending in half, and I have had the distinct feeling that this was as a result of them trying to become smaller - to become less noticeable and less of a target, even when they weren't necessarily under attack.

Many kids that I have worked with reveal their emotional state through physical changes in their neck. Whereas many kids get red in the face when embarrassed, some get red in the neck, with the skin reddening on one or both sides of the neck, but usually not in front. I have also witnessed children whose necks became so tight that I wondered if they were breathing. Sometimes I have seen neck veins pop out when a child is stressed or irritated, and in at least one case these responses were so severe that the child attempted to cover their neck by bending their chin toward their chest and resting their head in their hands. This was a clear indicator that the child was trying to shut down.

Law enforcement experts like Joe Navarro often look for tell-tale body language give-aways when questioning a person. One of the most common of these tells is rubbing the neck with one or both hands. A variation of this common cue of dishonesty or extreme discomfort is pulling the shirt away from the neck, as if in an effort to get more air, or as if the individual has suddenly overheated. Both of these behaviors extend to children as well.

I have also found that children are very clear when they are uncomfortable with the topic of discussion, or more particularly, with someone in the room. This is indicated by hugging their shoulders with both hands, either straight up and down with the elbows in, or by crossing the arms over the chest and grasping the shoulders. This is done while in a seated position or even while standing, and is a method of protecting the body's core. In most cases this type of body language is accompanied with a bent neck and lowered gaze.

On a more positive note, there is one posture involving the shoulders and neck that is generally a sign of playfulness, aloofness, boredom, or simply as a way to draw attention. This consists of the shoulders being rounded and pushed back, often with the arms on the hips, thighs, or even dangling at the sides, or grasped behind the back or around the back of a chair. This position exposes the body and is at the very least a sign that the child is fairly comfortable with their surroundings and/or the situation at hand.

4. THE HEAD & FACE

Just because we generally look other people in the face when we are talking to them doesn't mean that we are actually aware of what the body language in this region is telling us. But the fact of the matter is that there are many signals and cues that present in the face and head that can tell us a great deal more than whatever words are coming out of the person's mouth.

However, it should be noted that of all types of body language, facial movements and tells are the ones that most people consciously try to control. This is especially true of children who have had challenging or traumatic upbringings. These kids learn quickly to hide their emotional tells in order to adapt and survive the difficulties life has presented them. For instance, many traumatized kids learn to control signs of intense emotion;

quivering lips and jaws can be stayed, tears can be held back, gazes can be maintained or averted as needed.

Still, there are plenty of signs that are shown in the face and head that are completely subconscious, and a number of these are based on physiological responses to stress, fear or uncertainty. For instance, consider the physical processes that make a child (or anyone) blush. According to renowned blushing expert Ray Crozier, capillaries in the face - especially the cheeks - fill with blood and rise to the subcutaneous layers of skin, causing a distinct reddening of the face for many people. This is often associated with group scrutiny or being the focus of undesirable group attention, and Crozier is careful to point out that the blusher is not necessarily guilty of anything. (7)

But why is this? What involuntary physiological process makes this happen, and why did it evolve? If we assume that blushing had the evolutionary advantage of signaling visually what the blusher was feeling, then we must assume that this function is rather important socially and therefore it should be a sign that we take seriously in our roles as caregivers for children.

Other facial cues and body language are also based in evolutionary responses that defy culture. In fact, in a powerhouse article for the US Federal Bureau of Investigation titled *"Evaluating Truthfulness and Detecting Deception,"* several experts on body language postulate that all humans respond with the same type of facial responses to emotion, regardless of background, race, religion or any other demographic information. (8)

Thankfully, I don't need to explain all of the nuances that go along with the expression of emotion, as most people are naturally adapted to read facial cues, even if at a subconscious level. We all know what anger or sadness looks like, so what becomes more important is to learn the baseline behaviors for the kids we work with, and then use this knowledge to build a rapport that will help us recognize and quickly act when we see deviances from the baseline.

Ultimately, facial expressions are the ones most people learn to control, so it's best to use the wide range of other types of body language that are supportive of or at odds with what the child is saying and what their facial cues are indicating. This three-pronged approach to reading body language is especially effective when dealing with high risk kids.

5. RESPIRATORY

In all of my years working with kids, researching and writing about my field,

I have yet to hear someone talk about respiratory cues in relation to body language. But the fact of the matter is that the way people breathe is one of the most significant clues that you can glean from them about what they're really feeling.

In my time working with kids, I've noticed that the following types of breathing are indicative of certain emotions. Some of these may seem obvious, but the key here is to be able to recognize these breathing patterns even when they are not readily apparent or when the individual is attempting to control them:

*Broken breathing - may be an indicator of extreme emotion, or an indicator that the child may have been crying recently. Breath is focused mainly in upper chest and lower neck and may cause shoulders to quake or tremble. Gaze is often averted.

*Forceful breathing - may indicate anger, frustration or even rage about to emerge, but also might be produced when a child is purposefully trying to calm down. Breathing is pronounced and regular and is easily visible in the rise and fall of the chest.

*Hyperventilating - this type of behavior is often associated with anxious conditions and in some rare cases will result in the child losing consciousness. Because the breaths taken while hyperventilating are extremely shallow, it may be difficult to detect if a child is entering this state. Movement caused by hyperventilating will be focused primarily in the middle and lower abdomen.

*Sighing - when genuine, sighing seems to be a sign of reluctant but increasing acceptance, but it could also signal a child that has given up on the situation at hand. Breaths are deep and sometimes broken, with shoulders heaving noticeably.

*Cycling up - this type of breathing may indicate that the child is preparing to take specific action such as lashing out, destroying or throwing something, or bolting from the room/premises. Cycling up refers to forceful, deliberate breathing that becomes more forceful with more frequent breaths as the moment of action approaches. In most cases other body language has ceased, the gaze will remain highly fixated, and the neck and shoulders will be tense, as if readying to fight or take flight.

As usual, respiratory body language signals should be read in conjunction with other types of body language in order to gauge accuracy and honesty.

6. NO BODY LANGUAGE AT ALL

In some situations you may encounter a child that suddenly displays no body language at all. This could be attributed to what Joe Navarro calls the Freeze Response. According to Navarro, there is a key piece of the "Fight or Flight" response concept that is missing, and that option is to freeze.

Navarro argues that early humans were preyed upon mainly by beasts that hunted their prey based upon movement. Therefore, early humans evolved a response that caused them to freeze with the hope of remaining undetected and therefore unscathed in the event of a potential attack. (2)

If you work with high-risk, troubled or abused/neglected kids, chances are that you'll see this freeze response a lot in your career, and in my experience it is precisely as Mr. Navarro describes; a threatened child becomes immobile, exhibiting virtually no body language, frozen in place. This can come as a surprise because threats that we typically deal with in our line of work may seem innocuous to most, but to an at risk child, virtually anything can act as a trigger and set off the freeze response.

For example, calling a child into an office for a chat could be a fearful enough event (from their perspective) to elicit this response in a child or teenager, or it could be the result of the administration of a correction for negative behaviors. You may also see this response if the child in question is afraid of other children in the environment.

When you observe the freeze response in a child, you must change tactics immediately. Unfortunately, when a child is exhibiting the freeze response, many parents, educators and other caregivers mistake this behavior for passive defiance and consequently up the stakes by increasing the severity of the scolding or other consequences. But when a kid is legitimately frozen, this is probably the worst thing that you can do.

Instead, when you recognize the freeze response, it's best for you to do the same; stop moving, stop talking, sit down and relax. Lead by example and show the child how to use self-control to regain composure and overcome fears that are - in your protective environment - no longer in danger of becoming reality.

7. MIRRORING

We've all seen examples of mirroring; two friends leaning against a wall, arms and legs crossed, or a student assuming the same stance as his teacher. In institutional environments we often are able to tell a great deal about the social hierarchy of the kids we care for by observing their mimicry behavior. For instance, in a home for troubled boys, it can be easy to tell which boy is the leader of the group simply by watching the other boys mirroring him.

Some experts assert that mirroring is an important social function that is foundational to trust in human relationships (9), and I personally agree with this concept. In my experience people who are at odds with each other generally do not mirror each other (except in politics!), so I have often found this behavior to be a good sign when read in the correct context.

Mirroring is usually a subconscious act, although there are certainly people who attempt to manipulate this behavior artificially in order to affect their relationships and interactions with others. To be fair, some people also deliberately stage their own body language in order to achieve a certain effect, but it's safe to argue that most of the kids we work with will not be engaging in either of these behaviors deliberately.

The fact of the matter is that mirroring is usually a good thing and indicates some level of comfort between the parties. With kids, mirroring is a strong sign that the child feels comfortable or most identifies with the person who is "in charge" in the room, or sometimes the one who is currently speaking.

However, even in a negative context, mirroring can still be a good thing in that it can help direct us in our actions. For instance, consider for a moment that you are dealing with an unruly 13 year old boy who has attacked staff and other children during previous outbursts. You notice that another younger boy is mirroring the antagonist, which tells you that you need to redirect the situation immediately and separate those boys.

Or imagine that you're conducting a group meeting with several children and perhaps a couple of staff members. You might notice that a child who remains mostly quiet is mirroring one of the other staff members. In this case, it may be wise to arrange things so that requests for interaction come to the child from that particular staff member, as the mirroring behavior indicates some level of comfort, admiration or respect for the individual being mirrored.

NON-COMMUNICATIVE BODY POSITIONING

Recognizing the difference between body language - which is communicative - and body positioning - which is non-communicative - is a crucial part of fully "hearing" what a child is telling us. For instance, it's common knowledge that crossing the arms over the chest is a sign of resistance, standoffishness, or insecurity. While this may be true in some cases, other times this body position may be taken simply because the person is cold.

As another example, some authorities will tell you that talking with a hand over your mouth is a sign of deceit. However, I personally have known several good men who - especially during a scholarly conversation - would cover their mouth with their hand in a number of different ways. But for these men the position was merely comfortable.

There are many different reasons why a person holds their body in a certain way, and it isn't always a type of communication. Body positioning may be caused by discomfort, from being too cold, too hot, too tired, etc. As noted previously, it may also be a part of mirroring, in which case the more important focus should be on your body language, assuming that you are the lead in the interaction or the one being "mirrored."

So it's important not to attempt to read something into every movement. Distinguishing between body language and body positioning isn't always easy, but here again the key is to study the children that you work with; genuinely take interest in them, and you will quickly learn the difference.

Of course, analyzing the context of the body language after getting to know the child's mannerisms, character and general demeanor is ideal, but we must do so while keeping in mind that communicative body language is largely universal and mostly physiologically-based. This means that the most basic principles of comprehending body language are applicable even upon meeting a child for the first time, but are refined with each subsequent interaction.

KIDS IN CRISIS – THE CARRIAGE TIP-OVER STORY

Understanding body language is the framework from which Preemptive Behavior Therapy is applied. PBT is based on the natural evolutionary body language of an animal - man - as well as the specific body language of his varied cultures. Recognizing and interpreting this body language is essential in order to interrupt negative thought processes in children before those thoughts lead to negative actions.

In order to be successful applying the principles of PBT, you must recognize that moment where you can interrupt a child's progression toward negativity by distracting them even if only for an instant. In that instant you must seize the moment and redirect their energy and their thoughts while allowing them to quickly see how much better the results from this new behavior are for everyone as compared to what was about to happen.

With practice and consistency, in time we no longer have to be there in the "Flicker" moment. We don't need to continually interrupt the body-language-to-negative-thoughts-to-negative-action processes because eventually, the laws of conditioning set out by Ivan Pavlov and his Drooling Dogs come into play.

Just as Pavlov's dogs were taught at a subconscious level to produce a physiological response - drooling - upon hearing a bell with consistent conditioning, so too can children learn to interrupt their own thought process the moment their body begins to give advance warning through body language. With time and patience kids who are exposed to this method of behavior modification begin to redirect their own negativity before action occurs, and in many cases this is done subconsciously.

It's a beautiful system, but in order to understand just how critical these concepts can be in the right - or wrong - situation, I want to tell you a story about how a couple of horses and a newlywed couple were saved from almost certain doom as a result of the Flicker method. This case is especially poignant to me because the situation was extremely dangerous, and in my experience verbal communication changes under duress or while in crisis. This means that we must rely on other cues and behaviors in order to bridge the gap between doing what our emotions are urging us to do, and doing the right thing.

In February 2012 I was booked for a wedding with my horses and horse-drawn carriage. The venue was Montsalvat; an art community featuring a chapel and reception area that was quite popular for weddings.

Montsalvat lies on the side of a very steep hill. The Chapel is situated at the bottom of the hill, and a dirt road winds its way from the Chapel up to the reception area at the top of the hill.

On this day I took a beautiful team of identical coal-black Standard bred horses named Hawk and Eagle. I had worked with these horses for years in the city under chaotic and often confusing conditions. Working on the streets of Melbourne, Australia was a challenge; it wasn't like New York City where the horses work in the park, protected from the insanity of motorists, cyclists, pedestrians, road rage, crime, accidents and the stench of oil and gasoline. In Melbourne we were right in the thick of it; traffic and brakes and blaring horns and all.

I had a fantastic relationship with Hawk and Eagle, having spent months training them to recognize and respond to body language and verbal cues. It was blisteringly hot outside that day, and I had strayed slightly from the norm in that I had brought in a driver for the rig and I was filming the carriage and horses.

The bridal party entered the carriage outside the chapel; the groom, bride, 3 bridesmaids, 1 flower girl and 1 page boy: 7 people in the carriage, plus my driver. Not a load that my horses couldn't handle, but certainly a load that you want to be exceedingly careful with considering the grade of the hill leading to the reception area.

I remember saying to the driver;

"You need to move the horses into a fast pace to get up the hill, otherwise the carriage may start to lose traction and drag the horses backwards."

The Driver responded gruffly,

"I know how to do this."

With that the carriage rolled forward and off they went, but I saw rather quickly that there was going to be a serious problem if the driver did not heed my warning. Half way up the hill I observed the carriage faltering, so I yelled to the driver,

"You're going too slow; move the horses up!"

But the pace didn't change. Three quarters of the way up that behemoth hill the horses started to slide backward. I threw the camera down and rushed up the hill, but I felt like I was moving much too slow. I saw the horses begin losing ground; the driver then threw the reins and started screaming incoherently. At that point it appeared that my worst fears were being realized. The carriage began going back down the hill, dragging the horses with it. Screams from inside the carriage told me that the passengers knew they were in trouble.

I hollered at the horses to be heard over the commotion;

"Step up! Hold! Step up!"

But things only got worse when the strain became too much for Eagle and he fell to his knees. Hawk held fast but the whites of his eyes were flashing, nostrils flaring. Veins popped out in their necks, heads and backs as they put all of their effort toward self-preservation now; they both knew that if the carriage roared down that hill, there would probably be dead bodies at the bottom. I knew in that moment that both horses were only an instant away from panicking and losing all control.

But then a funny thing happened. Half resigned to catastrophe, I said a command in a reserved, quiet voice, and both horses turned one ear toward me. This meant that even in spite of the intensity of the situation, they were still listening to me; they still trusted me and that one little piece of body language told me exactly what I needed to do. During that one fleeting second where Hawk and Eagle locked on to me, time seemed to expand because a great deal happened during that instant.

To the right of the faltering carriage with its screaming wedding party was an old bluestone wall. It was about 2 feet high, and just beyond it was an area where the ground flattened out. I knew that we only had one more chance and that was to rip the carriage off the road, careen along and then jump off the wall and get the carriage turned around.

With those ears still turned to me, we made our move; I called out a simple, basic command that Hawk and Eagle had heard and responded to hundreds of times;

"G Orf!"

This command meant to turn sharp right, and because it was so ingrained in them, both horses acted simultaneously and rose together as one, pulling the carriage hard toward the rock wall. One of the wheels slipped on the embankment and for a terrifying moment I thought the entire group of horses and passengers were going to tumble down the hill, but I quickly instructed the team to go slightly left. They responded and righted the carriage just in time for me to finally reach them and grab the reins. At the last possible moment we jumped off the wall together, landing with an earth-shattering crash and coming to a stop on the flat area of ground I had seen while racing up the hill.

I applied the hand brake and checked the welfare of my passengers, but not before saying thank you to Hawk and Eagle for trusting me. Not long after, the wedding party emerged shaken but uninjured from the cabin and said their own thank-you's to the horses.

My point in telling you this story is that body language can tell us everything we need to know about what a child - or horse - is experiencing, and allows us to take the right action at precisely the right time. In the case of Hawk and Eagle, it was their right ears that had turned toward me that told me that despite the chaos of the situation, they were still listening to me and in this case, they were counting on me. They didn't know that they could get that carriage safely off the embankment, but they trusted that I knew.

So in my opinion, it was a combination of the Flicker and trust that prevented what could have been a deadly situation for 2 horses and at least 7 people. These lessons are easily transferred to kids, because as I have mentioned before, kids are indeed animals.

By studying the natural physical behavior of our kids and their body language, we can quickly assess a situation without needing to speak to the child, hear what has just preceded or anything else. When we know what these types of body language mean, they make monstrous and comprehensive statements that we can decipher with just a glance.

However, when you see these behaviors and physical cues, you must act! Don't sit there like so many other people I have seen in positions of authority and watch body language passively, waiting to see what the child will do next. Instead, ingrain self-correction in that child by interrupting the negative thought processes immediately and redirect/pre-correct the behavior before it ever occurs.

Using Hawk and Eagle as an example, the body language that indicated disaster was about to occur was the wild eyes and other fear-based body language that told me they were about to panic and bolt. If they had done so, all would have been lost. Thankfully, I was able to interrupt it because I knew the Flicker and I knew what to do when I recognized it, and the horses trusted me enough to respond properly.

When studying body language, there is an overall rule that tells us that sudden shifts in seating or standing position, such as a child suddenly sitting up and spacing their legs apart, or a receptive child that suddenly crosses their arms over their chest and becomes quiet, means that a shift in brain activity has occurred, and the body is preparing to take action in some way.

These transitional types of body language are the most pressing and immediate and should not be ignored. In fact, in my opinion it's irresponsible to ignore them, but far too many of the counselors, teachers and parents I have worked with do so.

You see that telltale rubbing of the neck or seemingly absent-minded covering of the mouth? Take action through redirection - mention that it's important and beneficial to tell the truth - virtually head off the lie that you see coming by the body language being used.

Notice a child who has shut down and is exhibiting the freeze response? You know what to do.

Witness mirroring between a female and male child? That's valuable information.

Observe a child in a group with their feet turned toward the door? You have a good idea of where they really want to be.

Hear a kid's breathing start ramping up, coupled with clenched fists and a fixated gaze? Time to intervene.

When you use the Flicker to interrupt negative thought patterns and emotions, over time the children you care for will begin to learn that you somehow know exactly how they're feeling, and that you usually also know just what to do to help them. This will build the level of trust between you strongly and quickly; often with surprising results.

The overall goal here is to create the Flicker by interrupting the thought process at the physical, evolutionary survival level, before the bad behavior has the chance to occur. Then help guide the child to allow themselves to believe that they corrected their own behavior, because in reality, they did.

References:

(1) Mehrabian, A. (1981). *Silent messages: Implicit communication of emotions and attitudes*. Belmont, CA: Wadsworth

http://www.kaaj.com/psych/smorder.html

(2) Navarro, Joe *Reserved Behaviors In The Study of Nonverbal Communications* Published on January 1, 2014 by Joe Navarro, M.A. in Psychology Today:
http://www.psychologytoday.com/blog/spycatcher/201401/reserved-behaviors-in-the-study-nonverbal-communications

(3) Navarro, Joe *Body Language of the Hands* Psychology Today - Spycatcher 01/20/2010
http://www.psychologytoday.com/blog/spycatcher/201001/body-language-the-hands

(4) Weinschenk, Susan *Your Hand Gestures are Speaking for You* Brain Wise in Psychology Today 09/26/2012
http://www.psychologytoday.com/blog/brain-wise/201209/your-hand-gestures-are-speaking-you

(5) Ahmad Ghanizadeh *Association of nail biting and psychiatric disorders in children and their parents in a psychiatrically referred sample of children* Child Adolesc Psychiatry Ment Health. 2008; 2: 13. Published online 2008 June 2. doi: 10.1186/1753-2000-2-13 National Center for Biotechnology Information
http://www.ncbi.nlm.nih.gov/pmc/articles/PMC2435519/

(6) Beth Haiken and Ann Bartz *Nail biting: Why it happens and what to do about it* Baby Center Expert Advice June 2012
http://www.babycenter.com/0_nail-biting-why-it-happens-and-what-to-do-about-it_65507.bc

(7) Crozier, W.R. *The Puzzle of Blushing* The Psychologist Volume 23 Part 5 May 2010 Pages 390-393
http://www.thepsychologist.org.uk/archive/archive_home.cfm?volumeID=23&editionID=188&ArticleID=1670

(8) DAVID MATSUMOTO, Ph.D., HYI SUNG HWANG, Ph.D., LISA SKINNER, J.D., and MARK FRANK, Ph.D. *Evaluating Truthfulness and Detecting Deception* Federal Bureau of Investigation June 2011
http://www.fbi.gov/stats-services/publications/law-enforcement-bulletin/june_2011/school_violence

(9) Kiderra, Inga Mirroring Might Reflect Badly on You July 28, 2011 University of California at San Diego, News Center
http://ucsdnews.ucsd.edu/archive/newsrel/soc/2011_07mimicry.asp

4 REDIRECTION

In the same way that we work to prevent negative behaviors from occurring, we also want to make sure that corrections only happen when necessary. To achieve this we use Redirections as a primary tool instead of Corrections. This is a critical distinction to make because most of the time we reserve corrections for when the negative behavior has actually occurred, which means that the correction by association is often a negative event.

Conversely, a redirection is often positive, or at the very least neutral and sometimes not even consciously noticed by the child. Redirection by its very nature occurs before the negative behavior takes place. So in order of general sequence and priority for the framework of Preemptive Behavior Therapy, we have:

*Body language is observed
*Flicker is achieved
*Redirection occurs
*Redirection Fails/Negative Behavior Occurs
*Correction occurs

A redirection can be as simple as a new line of discussion, or it can be as dramatic as removing the child from the environment. Whatever method of redirection you choose, it must be timed and presented in such a way as to interrupt the child's thought process and offer the child something new to focus on. When working with troubled and high risk kids, we must look at that momentary interruption as equivalent to the bell that Pavlov used to train his dogs; we can imprint a new behavior via the signal that we give immediately after the interruption.

If we imprint that interruption and new behavior cue consistently, the child will eventually exhibit the behavior of self-correction occurring at the subconscious level. This is the ultimate goal of PBT: to produce a child whose natural physiological and biological cues like body language send subconscious signals to the mental and emotional centers in the child's brain and central nervous system that causes an automatic self-correction.

However, here's the catch; in order to be able to imprint a child successfully in this manner, you must earn their trust. In the case of Hawk and Eagle and the wedding carriage, I was only able to prevent the disaster because of the mutual trust between those horses and me.

In that moment of extreme duress, all the horses could think to do was go directly forward, or at the very least to hold their ground. They essentially had blinders on in those moments, and therefore it never occurred to them to turn right off that low wall. But somehow I was able to spark the Flicker and redirected them with a simple, unexpected command that they trusted me enough to instantaneously follow. This event showed that the Flicker is an opening to engagement, and if you act quickly and rightly, you can use these principles to achieve astonishing results - even with very troubled kids and young adults.

But in order to recognize body language and behaviors in a child before negative actions occur and to be in a position to correct or redirect those behaviors, we must begin from a position of trust. In order to earn this trust and maintain your professional capacity, there are two central requirements:

1.) You Must Not Take Rejection Personally

Rejection is "par for the course" when it comes to gaining the trust of high risk kids. I learned this principle the hard way when my brother Mark died.

Mark had a beautiful Doberman Pinscher named Voss, and the two were inseparable. But Mark became very ill in his early thirties, and as his health deteriorated, Voss's psychological state deteriorated along with him. The dog became extremely nervous, anxious and flighty. It was evident that he could sense what was happening. When my brother went blind shortly before his death, Voss declined to the point that I knew it was time to take him home and help him heal. Mark died a month later.

When I brought Voss home he rejected me. He had no interest in becoming friends or even sitting together. Instead, he watched the entryway, waiting for Mark to come through the door to get him. But that day never came, and for a long time Voss would run to the window anxiously at the sound of every car, waiting for his master to return.

I watched him and waited. I wanted to love him so badly - he was all that I had left of my brother and it broke my heart to think of Voss being alone even though I was right there with him. At times I felt hurt that he would reject me; that he had no interest in me.

But I realized that his rejection was not personal. Instead, it was evolutionary. He had entered a type of survival mode in which he was maintaining a vigil. He believed that he was doing his job even when something deep inside of him told him that things were not right. So it wasn't that he didn't have interest in me specifically. He didn't have interest in anything. He was waiting, and grieving.

I gave Voss his space and it became much easier for me when I concluded that his rejection of me wasn't personal. And strangely enough, it was when I finally stopped taking his rejections personally that he began to come around more. He needed me to be the Alpha wolf, and my insecurity at his rejection was relegating me to a lower position that was confusing to a dog that had always had a stable partner in life. This made Voss even more anxious.

Voss came around when I relaxed and took a more professional approach to the problem. Likewise, if the child you're working with rejects you and you don't get emotional about it or take it personally, they'll see that you're cool under fire; that you are collected and resolute. These are the characteristics of a leader, and that's what Voss needed me to be, and that's what the kids we work with need us to be. You cannot be a leader when you are insecure about rejection; this places the rejecter in power, leading to confusion, anxiety and delayed trust.

2.) You Must Be neither Predator nor Prey

In my life I have spent a great deal of time traveling, working in the rings and fields with horses during the day and returning to isolated stables and barns late at night. I'm not afraid of much, but I recognized the benefits of having a canine companion to provide security and help me stay alert to any potential dangers.

So in 1998 I set out to meet a German Shepherd named Hamish that I had seen advertised for sale. This animal worked as a guard dog at a car yard that at one time had been the scene of numerous robberies. But word had it that since Hamish had been around, there hadn't been a single incident.

When I arrived at the car yard, I could easily see why. Hamish (in those days his name was Herman) rushed the gate at my presence, baring his teeth and growling viciously. He was remarkably aggressive and I hesitated for a moment as I felt a bit of fear rush into my heart.

But I quickly pulled myself together, not wanting to do anything to invoke this animal to become even more hostile. I realized I had actually jumped back in fear when Hamish charged the gate. This was not a good sign.

When the owner hurried to the gate moments later, I began to explain that the dog was simply too aggressive for me and that there was no possible way I could buy him. But as I was preparing to leave, Hamish caught my eye and a Flicker moment happened. We both stopped and observed the other carefully but not intensely. In those seconds I saw something in this animal that was extraordinary, but to this day I cannot describe what this was. I just knew that I had to act upon it, and before I realized what was happening I found myself asking if I could work with the dog for a few hours and see if I could get him to accept me.

The owner agreed and put Hamish on a long and sturdy lead, and I spent the next hour observing him. In return, Hamish observed me. He was no longer aggressive, but he was certainly not friendly. By the same token, he wasn't at all submissive or flighty. Instead, he acted as neither predator nor prey; not Alpha nor Beta.

I was so entranced with my careful and peripheral study of him that I didn't realize I too was acting virtually the same way, and it dawned on me that we were mirroring each other. I was also neither predator nor prey, Alpha nor Beta to Hamish. I was a curiosity to potentially be explored, and I felt pretty much the same way about him.

I took this mirroring as a good sign, as it's usually friends and people who respect one another who mirror each other.

After allowing Hamish to watch me from the end of his lead for some time, I then asked the handler to let him off the leash. He did so reluctantly, and Hamish trotted confidently toward me. As he approached I avoided eye contact with him but held my ground. He sniffed me and circled around me; watchful yet relaxed. His body language told me he was comfortable and when he finally pushed his muzzle into my arm, I knew that we had made an important connection.

The handler was frustrated with the fact that this process took a long time, but eventually admitted being surprised that the dog would accept a stranger so readily. I was surprised myself, but I attribute this success to the fact that I had acted rightly - partly by luck - during our encounter by being neither predator nor prey. This allowed Hamish the opportunity to observe and investigate me in his own way, and I believe that this is exactly the position we need to operate from when managing troubled kids.

However, it's critical to note that this took a significant conscious and focused effort on my part. Too often we get caught up in the emotion of an event and human nature takes over. When we react to situations emotionally, children sense this and though they may not know it consciously, they often interpret it as a deficiency because it's coming from an authority figure. Even at a very young age, children innately expect authority figures to be impartial because emotional investment in a situation means that a person is vulnerable, thereby weakening their position of authority.

We must retrain ourselves to appear as neither predator nor prey if we want to approach from a position of strength, and we must blend this position with the compassion that brings us all to this field to begin with.

REDIRECTION BEGINS AT A YOUNG AGE

A toddler cries because he cannot have a piece of candy, and so his parents quickly attempt to focus the child's attention instead on a shiny object and vigorously encourage him to interact with it.

This is an example of redirection; in this instance the child's behavior was corrected without the child even knowing that a "negative correction learning experience" had occurred. However, in this case the redirection has occurred after the negative behavior has already happened, which essentially means that this is a type of passive **correction** and not really a redirection for the purpose of this book.

But the point here is that we start conditioning children to respond to redirection early on. Then what seems to happen is that as children become more intelligent and better able to vocalize, we stray from this type of blatant distraction-type redirection. However, the principles of this can still be applied in a more progressive manner within the framework of PBT.

The following are the 11 primary types of redirection that must occur selectively depending on two conditions:

a. The principle negative action or behavior has not yet occurred
b. The Flicker has been achieved

If these conditions are met, one or more of these 11 redirections may be applied:

1.) Indirect Redirection - Present

One of the most effective types of redirection are indirect ones that seek to praise, encourage or otherwise point out exemplary behavior in another child who is present. For instance, if you are chaperoning a group trip to the park and you have one child who is exhibiting signs of withdrawal, it may be worthwhile to praise the efforts of a child who is being especially engaging and following the rules.

As another example, my editor is also a martial arts instructor who uses redirection to correct his students. If one student is performing a technique improperly, instead of correcting that student he will praise a child who is executing the technique properly. In most cases the child who needed the correction will then crane their neck around to see exactly what it is that the child who was praised is doing right, thereby leading to a form of self-correction.

Indirect redirections are passive but effective, allowing adjustments to be made to behavior without the child being aware that they have been corrected in any way. Keeping with the principles of PBT, this type of passivity leading to self-correction is a foundational concept and practice.

2.) Indirect Redirection - Absent

You can also use the indirect redirection with a party who is not present as the example. For instance, if you are talking with a child who is exhibiting body language that indicates they are lying, you can address this indirectly by mentioning the honesty of someone they respect. If you see the telltale signs of covering the face or neck, fidgeting or lack of eye contact, you could say something like;

"You remind me of XYZ. He is such an honest kid, and I think the two of you are a lot alike."

When using an absent third party as an example or model, it's important that the person be someone the child admires or respects, otherwise you run the risk of an aversive response to the example when presented.

3.) Direct Statement of Validation

Sometimes, a direct statement of what you think a child is feeling and validation of their emotions is the most potent method of disarmament available. If you recognize body language that indicates a child is feeling a certain way, in some cases you may find great success by coming right out and addressing this immediately;

"I know it feels like this isn't fair, and I can understand that. I know you feel like we're betraying you, and I want to work to assure you we're not."

Even when kids are hiding their emotions and thoughts, they usually don't want a complete breakdown of communication. So by saying what you think they are feeling and putting it out there on the table for them, they may feel relieved and validated, which will allow you to continue to improve the situation. In fact, sometimes, a direct statement or validation is all a kid really needs. They need to know that they have been heard, even when they're not being forthright with want they want to say.

4.) Direct Statement of Consequences

Kids often have difficulty understanding consequences when they are in the "heat of the moment." If you witness a child who is showing body language that you think is indicative that they are going to have a physical outburst, it may be wise to immediately redirect them with a direct statement of consequences.

"I can see that you're getting upset and I completely understand, but I need you to know that the consequences of acting out right now are XYZ."

This type of redirection lets you communicate that you are aware of where the general line of behavior the child is exhibiting is leading next, and that you want them to avoid the consequences of any outburst. This shows that you're looking out for their best interests even during times when they might not be very cooperative. But while it demonstrates that you care about the welfare of the child, it also clearly indicates that you must uphold the rules and any associated consequences for violations.

5.) Interjection

An interjection is a simple yet effective way to refocus a child and then redirect them into another line of thought. This must not be presented as an interruption in that the interjection must be related to the topic at hand in some way. For instance, if you are having a discussion with a child who is becoming more and more agitated about an altercation they had with another child, it wouldn't be wise to interject with a line of discussion about baseball.

However, it would be effective to interject with something more relevant, such as;

"My older brother used to get in a lot fights. Some he'd win and some he'd lose, but in most cases it wasn't long before he couldn't even remember what the fight was about. He came home with a major black eye one day..."

(This also utilizes item #7 below)

I have found that making your stories personal helps build credibility and trust. In this case the child will perk right up, soaking in the details of a brother who was a fighter, and staying interested long enough to hear your message whether they intend to or not: the fights were usually over nothing, as he couldn't even remember them later on. This is a subliminal way of saying that fighting just isn't worth it. But also, now they know a little piece of your history, and it humanizes you in their eyes.

Of course, this was a successful redirection, because the child is no longer getting amped up; they're now curious and interested in what you have to say, which is the perfect opportunity to continue redirecting them until they reach a calmer state.

The Abrupt-Segue Interjection

You can use an abrupt-segue interjection when it's your own words that are agitating, frustrating or otherwise bothering a child. For instance, let's imagine that you are in the middle of carefully spelling out a consequence for a recent outburst. Let's assume that consequence is a restriction of privileges. As you relay the consequence to the child, you notice body language indicating another outbreak may be imminent. The abrupt-segue interjection works like this:

"...and so Jenny, because of your outburst in the library, you'll need to re-earn your

privileges for next week - (At this point the child is becoming enraged and is about to lash out verbally or even physically) *tell me some of the first things you're going to do when you have full privileges again."*

This interjection arrests the child's line of thinking for three primary reasons;

a. You've clearly set the terms of the correction
b. You've focused the child's mind on the finite nature of the consequence
c. You've re-focused the child's mind on the good that is to come soon (insinuated; with good behavior)

In this particular case you'll likely already have the child's attention as they'll certainly be interested in whatever consequence you might be meting out, but you must achieve the Flicker moment before an outburst occurs. In this case you can use your own body language;

"...and so Jenny, because of your outburst in the library, you'll need to re-earn your privileges for next week -

And now you physically mark the abrupt segue interjection by raising a hand with one finger held up. This will stifle the child's immediate response to rebut, which is essentially a Flicker moment. Once you have that moment, you follow it up with something positive;

"tell me some of the first things you're going to do when you have full privileges again."

Important Note: An interjection should never be used to interrupt a child. True interruptions, where the child is in the middle of a line of thought or speech, are counteractive to a stable interaction and behavior. Whenever possible and appropriate, allow the child to speak their mind uninterrupted. This requires that you learn their body language and pay close attention to their speech and mannerisms so that you know when an appropriate moment to interject arises.

6.) Relation - Self

Children listen when adults they respect relate things personally, and there is no higher level of interaction between a child and a professional while in a professional setting. The relation of a personal story as a redirection is extremely effective when positioned properly, and is also a great way to quickly build trust and rapport.

However, it's important to ensure that the story you relate is very close to the target situation. For instance, let's imagine that you are observing a child who is extremely upset because he perceives that another child has received favored treatment; the two are arguing. You sense that an outburst of some type is about to occur, so you quietly step between the two and say to the antagonist;

"At one of my first jobs, my boss always seemed to favor another employee even though I worked just as hard. I'd get so mad, one time I almost quit! But later I found out that the other employee was putting in extra hours on the weekends and was working on a special project that I didn't know about. Turns out I was getting upset about something for nothing!"

In this case you have completely redirected the child's imminent negative behavior and thought pattern, shared something personal with them, and made is subtly clear that even you made mistakes, thereby hinting that the jealousy you observed may be unfounded.

You can also redirect a child who has withdrawn using this method - especially in cases where a child is becoming increasingly more withdrawn during a particular situation. You can capture the Flicker and arrest this descent with a personal story about how you relate to the child;

"When I was younger I'd run down to the barn to be with my horses when I got upset. They always made me feel better; it was so peaceful down there with them in their stalls, quietly chewing their hay. But even though it made me feel better, I still had to go back to face what I had run from in the first place, and sometimes that took a lot of courage."

Here the Flicker moment is captured when you tell the child that you - an authority figure - used to run away and hide when things got rough. That makes you human; it makes you like them, and therefore it makes you trustworthy. By relating a personal story of how you handled a situation where you were inclined to withdraw, you've effectively redirected the child's attention away from withdrawal and turned it toward interaction.

Of course, it's critical to remember that we must be careful what we reveal to the children we work with. If you work in an institutional setting, there are probably already specific guidelines in place in this regard. Otherwise, it's a matter of common sense that I can't do much to teach you in this book if you don't already have it.

7.) Relation - Consequence

In the same way that you can relate a personal story or make a direct statement of consequences, you can also relate a story about a third party who suffered consequences similar to what a soon-to-be-misbehaving child might suffer. This approach allows you to refocus the child's attention on a story about someone that they aren't necessarily attached to or personally know.

For instance, let's imagine that you have a child who is continually interrupting a group discussion or counseling session. Other attempts to redirect them have failed, at which time you relate a story about a child that once interrupted group sessions so often that they were restricted from attending any group functions for an extended period of time...including swim nights and pizza nights.

In this case you've made the redirection successful simply by the possibility of the potential consequence. Your short story related that there are positive benefits of the group environment that are worth preserving.

Making the story personal can be more effective, provided the negative behavior and associated consequence are fairly similar in content and outcome.

8.) Removal - Subject

In extreme cases it may be necessary to completely remove a child from the environment. This can be positioned in a number of ways, but the most successful way is to immediately suggest a change of scenery via abrupt but seemingly benign interjection;

"You know what, it's too noisy in here, let's go outside and go for a walk."
"It's more comfortable in the other room; let's go sit down."
"You want a glass of milk? Let's go in the kitchen."

However, in some cases a more stern removal may be necessary;

"You're disrupting the group; please take some quiet time for yourself now."
"In order to avoid serious consequences please go to your room for 30 minutes."

Suggesting or ordering a change of environment is a powerful type of redirection that can be used in a variety of different circumstances, but never with a child who is likely to self-harm in any way, and never without standard supervision protocols.

The transition time between environments is also an excellent cool-down period, and between the original distraction and this cooling time, it can be easy to use the Removal - Subject redirection to prevent a negative behavior from occurring.

If a child is removed from certain people or environments, it should be made clear that this is a temporary pause in their interactions and that you or other caretakers will be close by and checking on them regularly.

9.) Removal - Self

We are human, and therefore we make mistakes. We sometimes get emotional in front of kids. We sometimes betray our true state of mind with our body language. And occasionally, we feel threatened in certain situations. In any of these cases, it may be prudent to remove ourselves from a situation as a manner of redirecting the child in question, and as a manner of redirecting our own thoughts and emotions.

Self-removal can be as simple as walking into the next room, or even opening a book to signal you are momentarily done interacting with the child under the current conditions. In some cases, self-removal can be more serious if you have a child that is threatening - and capable of - committing acts of violence.

In any case, removing yourself from the situation should only be done when absolutely necessary, and only when there is adequate supervision in your stead. In times of imminent violence, you should immediately disengage and call for backup or assistance in the form of additional staff or adults and the police when necessary.

Your retraction from an interaction will serve to immediately refocus the child's attention and make it obvious that you will not continue to entertain their line of behavior, thus forcing them to change it if they want to gain your continued attention.

10.) The Sandwich

The sandwich is an easy way to quickly redirect a child whose body language or other traits indicate negative behavior is about to occur. The general idea is to quickly capture the Flicker by complimenting them, then "correcting them," and then finally complimenting them again. For example:

"Billy, I know you are very good at Xbox, but the other kids would like a turn too and I know that you are also really good at sharing."

"You put a lot of effort into your homework, Jenny, but if you worked on your long division more I think you'd be in top form as usual."

"You usually clean your room perfectly, Billy, and if you would just pick up these few things I think you'll have the cleanest room in the house."

"You're really good at sharing, Jenny; you could use a little work on not interrupting others, but your ability to express yourself is incredible."

The general formula here is Compliment-Correction-Compliment, where the first compliment provides the opportunity to capture the Flicker moment, the correction tells the child what you need them to do, and the second compliment reduces or eliminates any implied or actual negativity from the correction. It's a beautiful system, but we must be careful not to overuse this technique in a professional setting lest it becomes something that sounds canned and over-practiced.

11.) Intermission

Sometimes, the best type of redirection is a fun-filled intermission. In order to do this, you must have established trust with the child/children you are working with; otherwise, this approach may seem fake or insincere.

In my case, when I see a situation escalating between two or more kids and/or staff, I might call a "Dance Break!" in order to immediately gain everyone's attention and refocus it on something fun and positive by dancing around wildly for two or three minutes.

Not only does this provide a strong redirection, it also serves the purpose of exercise, which can help to diffuse any pent up anger or bad blood. Then when the break is over, the situation can be revisited and everyone involved will approach it from a different state of mind.

However, this technique doesn't have to be used only when things are getting heated. If you see a couple of kids lounging around, bored and starting to exhibit body language that trouble might be brewing, you can get them up and going and redirected by having a fun moment with them, with no strings attached. Spontaneity is a sign of trust and comfort, so if you are able to successfully use this method of behavior redirection with the kids you work with, then you're almost certainly doing something right.

Chapter Conclusion

Remember that the principle idea of the redirection is to *prevent* negative behavior from occurring - redirections are generally not intended to be used as a type of correction, or else the purpose of self-correction that we set out here to accomplish will become lost

After we gain even a miniscule Flicker moment, we use one or more redirections to change the child's thinking, refocus their thoughts on something else and avert the negative behavior that we predicted was about to happen based on our careful observations of body language and other cues. But most importantly, we must remember that redirections are all about timing. If you don't have the timing down, then you're not being observant enough, which means you have work to do.

Redirections are not always possible and/or plausible, and often negative behaviors will occur. For our purposes, we need some distinct methods of correcting bad behavior not in a finite sort of way, but in a preliminary way; meaning that the corrections we issue are only part of resolving negative behavior; the fundamental goal here is to teach the child to self-correct, which means that we need to use corrections appropriately and sparingly.

5 CORRECTIONS

Despite the best training and even with the most responsive children, not every redirection attempt will be successful. Sometimes, the impending behavior the redirection is working to prevent will occur anyway, and when it does your response must be appropriate and timely.

However, corrections are far more difficult than redirections, so there is additional motivation to learn how to make redirections work in addition to the principle concept of preventing negative behaviors or actions. Interestingly, some of the methods used for redirection can also be used post-behavior as a correction, but we must choose carefully from among the options for corrections for a number of critical reasons:

1. Corrections May Cause a Fight|Flight|Freeze Response in Children - Correct Correctly

Emotion plays a large role in whether a severe response is initiated, and a direct and immediate correction may be too frightening and/or intense for some children. They may respond with even worse behavior than your redirection and subsequent correction was meant to address.

This is because some traumatized, abused and neglected children automatically associate any type of correction with potential danger. Consider that many of these children were physically punished for infractions both real and imagined, which means that over time they develop a subconscious expectation that corrections will be emotionally or physically brutal.

Years later when these same children are under your care, they still respond emotionally to corrections because they have literally been trained to do so. Even if the child is cognizant of the fact that they are in no danger, the emotions that they feel when you correct them are still driven by subconscious expectations. This means that even a simple correction conducted incorrectly could cause a child to shut down, lash out or bolt from the room and possibly the premises.

Think of it like this; when you raise your arm to a dog that has been beaten, he will instinctively flinch, even if you are only raising your hand to get the dog's attention. Likewise a horse that has been bridled hard may jerk its head back reflexively even when you're reaching out to caress or give them a treat.

Consequently, corrections must be presented and timed appropriately. In doing so you will be building trust and eventually the subconscious emotional reactions will dwindle and even cease completely in some cases.

2. Disproportionate Corrections Cause a Loss of Trust

If the correction isn't proportionate to the behavior or pattern of behaviors in question, then the child will quickly learn to distrust you, and learned distrust is far more difficult to overcome than inherent distrust. A disproportionate correction is aptly classified as unfairness by children, which to them is a serious offense.

For example, if the behavior you are correcting is something as simple as a child cursing during playtime, but the correction issued is restriction of privileges for 2 weeks, this is a disproportionate response. Even if the child cannot fully articulate that they feel the correction is disproportionate, they will innately know that it is and will feel like you are a person who cannot be trusted because your responses are not logical.

This can be a difficult concept for some people to grasp, as many educators, counselors, support staff and caretakers think that a significant correction that is disproportionate to the negative behavior is a viable method of assuring compliance "next time." However, this generally is not how things work with troubled or high risk kids. Instead, the disproportionate response tells them that you do not act fairly, which means that you cannot be trusted.

3. Irrelevant Corrections Cause a Lack of Respect

If the correction isn't one that matters to the child, they will begin to hold you in contempt and will rapidly lose respect for you. For example, imagine the correction that you issue to a child who is acting out in a group setting is to send them to their room. However, this child relishes alone time and doesn't really mind being separated from the group. In fact, it's probable that the acting out is a subconscious manner of extrication from the group setting, and if this type of irrelevant correction is repeated enough times, the child will learn to deliberately act out in order to be sent to their room.

What this and other situations like it tell the child is that you can be manipulated, and few children respect adults that they can exert noticeable and deliberate control over. This loss of respect can make it difficult to discipline the child in other ways. Therefore, the correction must be something that the child cares about.

4. Unrelated Corrections Cause Confusion and Loss of Trust

In the example in item 3 above, though the correction is irrelevant in that it doesn't really bother the child, it is still a correction that is *related* to the behavior and therefore it makes sense; "if you act out in a group setting, you are removed from the group."

But if the correction isn't really related to the behavior, the child will begin to lose trust in you as a result of your seemingly illogical correction.

For instance, imagine that a child has been neglecting their household chores. You issue a correction in the form of a direct verbal admonishment coupled with a revocation of privileges to attend a special group function at the end of the week.

In the child's eyes, the behavior and the correction are unrelated. And if corrections and consequences don't make sense to a child, they will begin to question you and lose trust in you. Instead, in this situation the correction should be something related; additional work or community service, temporary restriction of in-house privileges until chores are completed, etc. If the correction is related to the behavior, the child will more readily understand and correlate the two and the path to achieving self-regulation in this regard will be that much shorter and easier.

CORRECTION TYPES USED IN PBT

There are two primary types of correction. In cases where the act of *redirection* does not also cause a *correction*, then a direct or indirect correction may be required - especially if the impending negative behavior occurred in whole or in part.

Direct corrections refer to corrections or consequences that are high impact, and as such they have the most potential for causing an additional outburst of bad behavior or a fight/flight/freeze response. Direct, high impact corrections should generally be considered Elevated Corrections and should only be used where indirect corrections have not worked in the past or cannot be applied to the particular situation in question.

Indirect corrections are considered low impact and present the least chance for a fight-or-flight disturbance. These types of corrections are soft and/or passive when possible and should be used as a first option after a redirection has failed and a negative behavior has occurred.

However, it should be noted that some children might perceive indirect, low impact corrections as high impact, fear-inducing events. For instance, consider a child whose history includes severe parental neglect. If you direct this child into a "time out" for negative behavior, you might consider this a low impact, indirect correction, while this particular child might perceive it as the worst consequence possible and see it as something akin to neglect.

Special situations like these only solidify the idea that we must study the children in our care and actively work to gain their trust by being aware of their particular life history and challenges. So while I would love to say that all of the tenets of Preemptive Behavior Therapy will work with every child, this is just not possible. You must think and work outside the box and strive to give and earn trust and respect.

Specific Correction Types Used in Preemptive Behavior Therapy

INDIRECT CORRECTIONS

*Time Out

The time-out is a classic de-escalator. It's considered an indirect correction because all potential antagonists are removed from the presence of the child. The child can then take time to cool down without the stress of the unwanted presence of another child, staff member, or you. This also permits ample time for reflection on the issue, allowing the child to process things in a relaxed state.

A time-out does not mean that a child must be alone. A time-out should be a fairly quiet place, but can be within view of a guardian. It can also be in the child's bedroom if they can be trusted to be alone while upset. The primary goal of a time out is to ensure that the child does not interact with anyone negatively.

Where many parents and caretakers go wrong is when they assume that a time-out must preclude any type of activities. The idea of a time-out for many people means the child is supposed to "just sit there and think about what you did."

I disagree. A time-out should be taken more literally; it is time away from a particular situation or interaction. If there is a book the child would like to read while in time-out, let them. If they prefer to draw or play music, let them. If they would like to play quietly with toys, let them. No television or movies, and no computer time unless there is no connection to the internet.

A time-out should be used wisely. If the child wishes to do something to further their intelligence or refocus their disposition, they should be free to do so. Forcing a child to sit in a chair and do nothing for 15, 20 or 30 minutes is a wasted correction, because the child can't possibly think only about the particular situation in question and nothing else for that long. And if they do, then they're probably not going to calm down as quickly, because you're forcing them to do nothing but think about it. In this situation, if they thought you were being unfair before, now they're going to think this even more while they stew on it.

A child will think about the negative event in their own way and in their own time. They can do so while playing quietly, while reading a book, while drawing, etc. In fact, you should encourage them to develop an outlet like these to funnel negative energy into something positive, which will help the child to process the situation from an entirely different frame of reference.

I will say this again; use time-outs wisely.

The time-out also allows you and other caretakers vital time to regroup and consider the best course of action going forward. And after especially intense behavior violations, it can also give you a chance to get your emotions under control. We are all human, after all.

*Correction by Proxy

Sometimes when negative behavior is occurring we don't need to correct the child directly or even address them at all. Instead, we can praise one of their peers who are behaving correctly. This can be extremely effective when the child exhibiting the exemplary behavior is present, although it can also be effective when the example child is not present.

The idea is to genuinely praise a child who is behaving correctly. For instance, if you have several children on a group outing and one is misbehaving, instead of addressing them directly you can praise a child who is behaving well. So if Billy is breaking rules and/or misbehaving, you can turn to Betty and say;

"Betty, thank you so much for being such an excellent role model today!"

This alone may cause Billy's attention to refocus on behaving better because he desires praise more than he desires redirections, admonishments or corrections.

You can also praise or use as an example a child who is not present, but who the misbehaving child has some respect for. As an example, if Billy is misbehaving but you know that he admires the slightly older and more mature Phillip, then you can say something like;

"You know, Billy, one of the reasons that Phillip has been doing so well lately is because he doesn't engage in behavior like this."

You can even try;

"Would you be acting like this if Phillip was here right now?"

Or;

"Billy, stop for a moment and ask yourself how someone like Phillip might handle this situation. Would he do it differently, do you think?"

I am a huge fan of asking children questions instead of lecturing them or barking out instructions and information. Instead, I gently require them to think it out and come up with their own conclusions. Self-realized, these conclusions are more valuable and relevant to the child than the same conclusion directed at them by you or another adult or authority figure. This is a critical part of self-regulation and self-correction and is one of the fastest methods I know of whereby you can quickly and radically change a child's way of thinking and associated behaviors by allowing them to feel fully empowered by coming up with the answers on their own.

Because after all, we need to empower these kids more than anything else. It's their best chance for a happy and fruitful life, because to feel empowered is to live powerfully.

*Correction by Example

Children respond well to personal stories or examples that are relevant to them or just plain interesting. This means that you can relate to them stories about how you or someone you know have been in similar situations and how they responded, and what the consequences or benefits of those responses were. This purchases time that can be used to de-escalate the child and refocus their attention, and it also builds trust if your stories or anecdotes are honest.

For instance, let's imagine that you have a child who struggles with anxiety. In this particular case they're being defiant about taking part in a required group activity. If you also experienced anxiety in your life, it's okay to tell them this and in fact you can quickly build trust by sharing with them in this way.

"You know Erica; I used to suffer from bad anxiety too. I was afraid to go out and do things, but then I missed out on some of the best things in life. I have a few methods of dealing with anxiety that really work; do you want to try them with me?"

Or, you can relate a story about someone you know who suffered from anxiety and how they dealt with it. This is an indirect type of correction because you are first sharing something about yourself or someone you know, which helps to build trust, and then you're also helping the child to refocus their behavior. This essentially means that you have created a Flicker moment and can change the course of the child's behavior in a rather low-impact way that is free from consequence.

Of course, it's vital that everything you say to a child is true. Don't make up stories solely for the sake of teaching a lesson or correcting a behavior. My theory is that all people - children included - subconsciously pick up on lies, half-truths and embellished stories, and this can affect your relationship with them. But more importantly, we are trying to teach them to be good, thoughtful and honest people. Why would they take these lessons seriously if we're making things up just to prove a point? Ultimately, if you can't relate to a child in this way, don't use this method or correction. Find another way.

*Writing Task

This is one of the most powerful indirect types of corrections that I know of. It's largely unconventional, but it works for a number of very sound reasons.

First, assigning a child a writing task related to their negative behavior means that they will have plenty of time to calm down and think things through considering that you must give a child exactly 24 hours to deliver on the writing assignment. This is because after 24 hours they begin to forget the specifics of the sequence of events that led up to the negative behavior event, but earlier than that time frame and the moment may still be too "fresh" for the child. Setting the delivery time for the writing piece at the same time the next day helps solidify the impact of the consequence because you are partly recreating the events and sending a subconscious signal; the time of behavior and the time of official correction - the submission of the paper - are subconsciously integrated.

Second, you internalize things differently when you write about them. Seeing your thoughts, memories and behavior on paper changes your views of them and forces you to discuss them in simple terms.

Third, the writing task provides you with an opportunity to praise the child for their work, which helps to promote the idea that corrections are not necessarily a bad thing. Instead, they are merely learning experiences. You can also use this writing task later on to remind a child about the consequences of continued bad behavior.

Finally, you can glean a wealth of information from what a child writes, but it's important that you not think of the writing task as a punishment - it is not. Assigning a child a task to write meaningless/unrelated essays or to simply write the same "I will not repeat this behavior" line hundreds of times is not the idea here. Instead, you should ask the child to write about the sequence of events that occurred leading up to and including the negative behavior. The final part of this paper should include the child's thoughts about what could have been done differently to avoid the negative behavior.

Upon review of this paper you'll have a clear idea of the child's thought process leading up to the behavior and will have a calmly composed version of the event which can help you understand what they were thinking at the time and why they chose the particular actions they engaged in. This is extremely valuable information.

Just be certain that proper spelling and grammar isn't the major focus of this assignment. Instead, the exercise in articulation is the primary task. However, if you have a child who is receptive, you can also use the opportunity to help them brush up on their communication skills - the most important tools that we possess as humans.

*Refer to Higher Authority

Sometimes you may not have the clout (or respect) needed to properly correct a child. You could be a new staff member or educator, the child could be new to your facility, or the child might have a direct personal problem with you, rendering your authority less valid.

One very firm but still indirect way of correcting a child's behavior is to refer them to a "higher authority," or someone that does hold the necessary clout and respect with the child to be taken seriously as a potential source of conflict.

For instance, if Billy is misbehaving and other techniques do not work, you could refer him to, say, your supervisor Peter in the home for adolescents you work in.

"Billy, I can see that I'm not getting through to you right now, so I'm going to have no recourse but to talk to Peter about this."

Or, if the behavior has not yet escalated sufficiently for this, you could try a more preventative approach;

"Billy, you seem to be struggling to self-regulate your behavior right now. Can you bring it back under control so that we don't have to involve Peter in this?"

It's important that whomever you "refer" Billy to is someone that the child trusts and respects, but is also someone who takes a different approach to situations than you do, thereby for whatever reason commanding more respect from the child than you at the moment.

The idea of escalating a situation to a higher authority is one that even the most unruly children often respond to, either immediately or delayed, but the primary goal for you is to use the tactic to immediately cease the behavior, showing that you have control of the situation despite the lack of respect...and in return, the child may come to respect you.

DIRECT CORRECTIONS

*Time In

A time-in is a direct correction where you and the child in question immediately stop whatever you're doing and quietly sit in the same room together for a specific period of time. The space used for this must not be a high traffic area and it must be cleared of other children and adults if possible, unless they are involved in the events at hand.

The setting for a time-in works something like this. Imagine that you witnessed body language indicators that told you Billy was about to lash out at another child. You attempted to redirect him using an interjection type redirection that failed, after which time Billy lashed out at the other child. You immediately call "Billy, Time-In!" and ask the other people in the room to leave. You explain to Billy that the two of you will simply sit in silence and relax for 5, 10 or 15 minutes.

Ideally, you will try to capture a Flicker moment in order to proceed from the time-in. You can easily do this with an icebreaker such as a joke or a funny story, but one of my favorites is to restart the dialogue by apologizing, and I always mean it;

"I'm sorry that just happened Billy, and I'm looking forward to moving past it with you."

I am sorry that it happened, so the apology is genuine.

*Direct Verbal

A direct verbal correction is tough love at its finest. With this type of correction you immediately point out the behavior and require that it change in very simple terms.

"Billy, what you're doing right now is not okay, and it needs to stop. Let's go for a walk and chill out for a bit."

In this case you were very direct with the child, which in itself is a sufficient and memorable correction when done skillfully. But you also incorporate a redirection post-correction, which likely captured a Flicker moment by refocusing the thought pattern of the child to the walk. Now, the walk itself will allow you to physically calm the child, refocus their attention via new surroundings, and reinforce the trust you are working on. This trust tells the child that you are legitimately concerned with their welfare, but that you will require them to behave appropriately.

A less direct form of the direct verbal correction - and one I prefer - is to immediately stop the child and query them about their behavior:

"Billy, do you think what you're doing right now is okay?"

This also acts as a redirection because it forces the child to reframe what's going on - they're not being commanded or lectured, they're being treated with respect in the sense that their opinion is being asked. Of course, if you ask a question like this, you must allow the child to answer.

*Direct verbal with Consequence

The title of this section is clear; when a negative behavior occurs that warrants such a high impact response, you can directly and immediately address the misbehavior and introduce a consequence simultaneously.

Revisiting the example above, the technique would be modified;

"Billy, what you're doing right now is not okay, and it needs to stop. You need to go sit in time-out for 20 minutes."

This correction would be appropriate for when a direct verbal correction isn't enough. However, it's important to review the fact that man is an animal, and animals respond to certain stimuli in specific ways. Children easily learn from verbal corrections when they are issued logically and fairly. This means that in many cases, an additional consequence isn't necessary.

Of course, this is the ideal but not necessarily the norm. The point is that if you can issue the correction without the additional consequence, you should. Solving issues using communication will allow you to build added trust with the child, and demonstrates that you are even-handed.

MIXED CORRECTIONS

Re-Earning of Privileges

In my experience, the loss of privileges is the most common type of correction. However, it is necessary to reframe this concept as a re-earning of privileges. By their very nature privileges are not rights and must be earned, so by asking children to re-earn privileges, it signifies immediately that:

1. The correction is temporary
2. The child has control over the situation

Privileges can range from video game time to television to special events, outings and "hanging out," telephone or internet privileges, and many others.

In the case where a negative behavior has occurred and the privilege loss is something the child won't directly experience until a time in the future, then the correction is considered indirect. If the privilege loss is something the child will directly deal with immediately, then the correction is considered direct, which also means that it is high impact and should be reserved as a step-up in intensity from an indirect correction.

For example, if a child engages in negative behavior and you issue a correction that he/she cannot go on a special outing the following week, this is an indirect correction. But if the correction is an immediate loss of phone or internet privileges, this is an example of a direct correction. In either case there should be a built-in way for the child to earn back some or all of these privileges.

Whether direct or indirect, the most effective types of privilege loss/re-earning corrections are those that are closely related to the negative behavior. For instance, in the case of the loss of a special outing, the associated behavior should be something like disrupting a group meeting, fighting, or something similar. In the case of the loss of phone privileges, the associated behavior should be something like cursing or other vocal offenses, inattention, or violations directly related to use of the phone.

The old saying *"Let the punishment fit the crime"* holds largely true here as well.

Community service

Community service is an excellent motivator for good behavior and makes for a versatile type of correction. Community service can be related to the negative behavior, such as assigning extra chores when something a child does makes a particular mess, or it can be loosely related. For example, imagine that a child under your care has struck another child. Other correction types have not worked in the past, so you assign 20 hours of community service at a retirement center. The justification for this correction is that physical violence isn't just a crime against another person -

it is a crime against society. When we strike someone, we make them a victim, so the correction in this case is for the child to be responsible to and help others who are vulnerable; namely, the folks in the retirement home.

There is a related type of community service that can be assigned to help correct nearly any negative behavior, and in most cases you'll be able to clearly articulate the association to the child. However, this may involve some legwork and community involvement on your part.

I have heard some argue that community service should not be used as a correction because it jades the child's view of volunteer work, but I argue the exact opposite. I have seen children assigned to community service that learned, grew and changed as a result of their service, and some who even benefitted financially with a new skill or career path learned while performing community service.

Ultimately, the social aspect of community service performed well can negate the entire idea that the service was assigned as a correction to begin with, and can result in a child who becomes hungry to help others.

Four Key Things to Remember About Corrections

1. *Never Threaten; Always Predict*

This is extremely important; you must never *threaten*. A threat is something that you may or may not intend to follow through with. Instead you must predict; if item A happens, item B *will* be the result. This means that you must stick to your word. If you advise a child that the result of an impending negative behavior is a specific correction or consequence and that child engages in the behavior anyway, then you must follow through and administer the correction you predicted.

Trust is associated with consistency, and if you are consistent in your interactions with a child, then you will build enough trust with them that they will adjust their behavior based upon your need to issue predictions. If you are consistent in this regard, it is possible to detach yourself from the correction entirely, meaning;

"Billy, I am merely advising you of what you already know will happen if you do XYZ."

This is sort of like if you advise Billy that jumping in a flooded river will result in his drowning; it's not you who caused the consequence; you are merely the messenger.

2. Corrections are Future Redirections

Each correction that you make with a child is actually a future redirection. This is because when you observe body language indicators that tell you a child is about to do something they shouldn't, you can redirect them with an interjection reminding them of "what happened last time," and provide them with a reminder of what they need to do in order to avoid this.

Ultimately, this means that today's negative behavior can literally prevent tomorrow's negative behavior, and this is a concept that is okay to share with the child if they are capable of understanding it. You can best impart this idea to them by explaining post-correction that making mistakes is a part of learning, and when we learn from our mistakes, we grow. Therefore, there's no need to make the same mistake twice when you already know what the consequences will be.

3. Corrections must be Individually Tailored

All too often I see teachers, clinicians and many other people who are responsible for the welfare of high-risk kids apply cookie-cutter routines, behavior expectations and consequences. In my opinion this does not serve children well and isn't very efficient. Not every correction type will work with every child, therefore it's perfectly natural - and expected - that you tailor behavior programs to the individual child.

4. Corrections Should Follow the Order of Least Restriction

Corrections should always follow a natural order of least restriction. Restrictive practices should be reserved for times when other corrections or redirections are not possible or likely to be effective. When restrictive practices are used, they should be temporary in nature and the child should clearly understand what is required in order to re-earn privileges or otherwise lift those restrictions.

A PERSONAL STORY OF TRIUMPH

I once had a highly disturbed young man in my care. He was aggressive, violent and extremely unpredictable. Several professionals had advised me that in their opinion, the child was virtually destined to become a killer, and on one occasion the boy told me himself that *"the urge to kill in me is strong."*

But early in our relationship I had caught a Flicker moment with the child, and I found my way through his defenses because I was consistent, honest, friendly but fair and kind but firm with him. He had been out of control for so long that he was not accustomed to someone holding their ground in the face of his intense outbursts. When I held my own I earned his respect, and when I refused to lie to him or candy-coat things, I earned his trust.

Eventually, he began to crave rules and structure in his life. He wanted to know the right way to do things and to be recognized when he did them well. He wanted consistency and respect, and he got it when he gave it. It took a couple of years, but in time he changed so much that today he is not at all the same young boy I met so long ago.

Recently I received a letter from my former ward. He is now a grown man and has entered and is living in the world the right way, and he attributes this to the things he learned while under my care.

I was once asked what specifically it was that I did in order to help this boy turn his life around, and my answer is in this book. While I might not have had things organized or spelled out in detail, the principles here are the same principles that changed this boy from a potential killer to a kind human being contributing the best he can to his community.

What I did with this child was nothing more than what I am detailing in this book; I learned body language and studied his in particular. I caught Flicker moments and redirected his behavior when I could. I corrected negative behaviors when I was forced to. And all the while, I was honest about what I was doing; I told him many times that I wasn't the one doing the hard work - I told him that in fact he was the one doing the heavy lifting, while I was merely guiding him on *the path to self-correction.*

So the truth is that I didn't win this young man's battle for him. He won it for himself, and I had the honor of being there to coach him on his way. As practitioners of Preemptive Behavior Therapy, this is our primary role. We are not leaders and we are not teachers. We are only guides who walk beside our children for a short while in this life.

6 REWARDS

Animals thrive on rewards. From training chimps to operate complicated machinery to teaching dolphins how to disarm underwater mines, humans have demonstrated that the reward system is something that deeply impacts behavior. In fact, rewards affect animals at the biological level - as seen in the case of Pavlov and his drooling dogs, where the consistent reward of food "programmed" the dogs to salivate at the sound of a bell; later even when there was no food present.

In the ring we train horses using a combination of techniques, including offering rewards in the form of small treats from time to time during a training session. Dog handlers and trainers use similar techniques blended with enthusiastic praise. Certain species of birds are trained to solve puzzles and other logic-based games and tasks, and in many cases they are rewarded with treats, and always with praise and affection for a job well done.

Now, as I have mentioned before, we tend to forget that as humans we are in fact animals. We are not somehow outside of the realm of nature - on the contrary; a great deal of our suffering as a society is due to the denial of the idea that we are animals and that we have innate behaviors and feelings that we sometimes cannot explain.

Because we are animals we respond well to rewards, and this is especially true of children and impressionable teens and young adults. However, our view as a society of what constitutes a reward - and when to award them - is more than a little skewed. As detailed below, a reward can be something as obvious as a mini candy bar, or something with a lower profile like the release of pressure.

But before we get into the types of rewards used in Preemptive Behavior Therapy, I want you to consider how addiction works. In very basic terms, what happens is that drugs interact with neurotransmitters in the brain in such a way that causes a state of euphoria or other desirable effects. However, believe it or not, it's not drugs like heroin and meth that people become addicted to; it's the release of or interference in the function of neurotransmitters that the drug causes that is addictive.

Heroin, for example, causes these interactions at a grand scale resulting in total euphoria - which is precisely why it is so addictive. But other things besides chemical substances activate the reward pathways in the brain and affect neurotransmitters, and this includes rewards.

In order to demonstrate this, if we follow the addiction scale down the ladder of severity, we might see something like this:

Heroin/Meth/Crack

Alcohol/Tobacco

Gambling

Sex

Gaming/Internet

Eating

So we know that people can become addicted to many different activities, substances, experiences and emotions. All of this is possible as a result of the way humans are pre-wired to respond to rewards; each of the items listed cause a feeling of satiation, happiness, pleasure or euphoria, which means that they trigger potent reward pathways in the brain and central nervous system.

I want you to think about how powerful this system is, because you can (in effect) use it to help a troubled child or teen become "addicted" to the rewards associated with good behavior. These rewards can be tangible such as a small piece of candy or a special trip, or they can be intangible like the feeling of pride that comes with acting rightly, when rightness is recognized and groomed as desirable. This means that you must develop a system of rewards that are individually tailored to each child, and you must employ this system consistently.

The interesting thing about this process is that it becomes nearly as rewarding for the caretaker as it does for the child. When you begin to see the effects of behavioral interdiction, positive reinforcement and consistent, reasonable rewards, the sense of pride and community accomplishment is itself a significant reward that you will come to crave and repeat.

By rewarding others, we reward ourselves.

Rewards as Redirections | Corrections

In the same way that a redirection can serve as a correction, a reward can also serve as a correction. While these might seem like opposing concepts, the application of a reward as a redirection or correction is achieved in a similar way. Consider the following situation:

Becky is misbehaving in a group setting. At this stage you recognize body language indicators that are a sign of imminent escalation. Your immediate attention should now be focused on achieving the Flicker and issuing a deft redirection. Or should it?

In some cases, it may be more efficient and effective to reward a child who is behaving correctly than it is to redirect or correct a misbehaving one. In this situation, you can achieve the Flicker by presenting a small reward to Jessica, who is exhibiting desirable behavior. This will immediately focus Becky's attention. The redirection is then achieved by thanking and/or praising Jessica for her good behavior.

With luck and skillful application, in this case you were able to accomplish both a redirection and a reward with one action and without creating any type of negative "correction event." Even though your intention was to redirect or correct Becky's behavior, by rewarding Jessica instead, you clearly demonstrated to all present exactly what type of behavior is appropriate and worthy of reward, without reprimanding, embarrassing, or calling anyone out in any way.

In Becky's mind, the message is clear; this behavior is what is expected, and this is what Becky can expect if she behaves similarly. Ideally, Becky will adjust her behavior accordingly with the correct impression that she self-regulated her behavior.

Using a reward as a correction is PBT at its finest, but this is just one small example. With a little ingenuity, there are numerous ways that you can adapt and apply this concept to your particular teaching or behavioral model. Considering that I have applied this technique both with horses and dogs, I am certain that you will be able to personalize and improve upon the basic foundations that I've laid out here, as we all respond to rewards in generally the same way.

So keep in mind that a reward is not always *just* a reward. It can be much more than that.

Types of rewards:

RELEASE OF PRESSURE

I'm listing this reward type first because it's likely to be the most difficult to understand for some people. Release of pressure can be something as simple as excusing a child from the room, or it can be as complicated as an integrated, incremental restoration of privileges after a major correction. To best explain how the release of pressure can be used to help guide children on the path toward self-regulation, it's necessary to travel back to my equestrian roots.

A few years ago I traveled to the U.S. to work with and become certified by Ed Thornton; the only triple-certified John Lyons Conditioned Response Trainer in the world. An American horse trainer, Thornton is a renowned natural horseman who taught me some fascinating principles of working with horses that focus on applying proportionate pressure while maintaining personal space.

Thornton essentially taught that while it's not possible for one person to physically move an 1800lb horse, it is possible to move the tip of an ear, a hoof, or some other small but significant portion of the horse's body or demeanor. This coincided beautifully with my Flicker theory, whereby I could move an animal that was much larger than me if I could interrupt its thought process and redirect its behavior.

But when Thornton explained Lyons' ideas of proportionate pressure and personal space, it occurred to me that these same principles would hold true in practice during my work with troubled, disadvantaged and at-risk youth. To summarize how this horse training can be applied to our roles as caregivers, educators and parents, we need to understand the following and hold this principle dear in all that we do:

"Our responses must be proportionate while applying exactly the right amount of pressure in order to elicit the desired behavior."

This is no easy task for anyone, but in our case, why not "move" an ear with a candy bar? Why not move a pair of eyes with a thumbs-up? Why not move one child's entire body by rewarding another child? Rewards are often not what you're accustomed to - they can be anything that means something to a child, including the release of proportionate pressure, or more specifically; the release of a redirection, easing or retraction of a prediction of consequence, or the release of an actual correction/consequence.

Remember that we are animals that respond to even the slightest rewards, but we must still be proportionate in our interactions with the kids we work with. By being proportionate, we automatically maintain personal space physically and emotionally, and it is this that allows us to accomplish our job professionally while still humanizing us in the eyes of those we work with. Conversely, if we are not proportionate in our response, we risk losing all credibility and trust, and in my experience this can happen quickly if you're not observant and ambitious.

REVERSAL OF CORRECTION

This reward is unique in that it can be offered at the time of correction. For instance, when you issue a specific correction - such as a loss of telephone privileges - you can soften the correction into a redirection by informing the child that if they meet your behavior requirements or other conditions, the phone privileges can be restored early.

In fact, this is a practice often used in court systems in the United States, Britain and Australia. In some cases, upon conviction a judge or magistrate will dictate that with good behavior for a set period of time (usually one year or more), the conviction will be expunged from the person's record.

In other cases jail or prison sentences may be handed down, but suspended based on good behavior.

You can apply a reversal of correction either immediately or gradually as a method of rewarding a child for improved behavior or for meeting other conditions. While it might not appear so on the surface, this is indeed a powerful type of reward and a highly effective method of behavior modification leading to self-governance.

It is also possible to use a reversal of correction as a reward after the correction is already ongoing. For instance, if a child has been restricted in some way for a period of 7 days as a result of some infraction or outburst, you can reduce that time or eliminate it unexpectedly as a reward for good behavior.

Let's go back to our case of Becky and Jessica, but this time let's assume that Jessica has been on restriction for certain privileges. The consequences of her negative behavior were 7 days of restricted phone, television and computer/internet privileges. But when Becky is acting up and you need to carefully redirect her, you can do so by rewarding Jessica, something to the effect of;

"Jessica, you're doing a great job by setting the example here today among your peers, so as a result I'm going to eliminate the remainder of your restriction period."

In this case you have rewarded Jessica for her good behavior and redirected Becky for her negative behavior with one efficient and positive action.

Of course, the problem with this method of reward is the danger of undermining your own authority, or worse - that of a colleague. This means that the reward must legitimately be warranted by the desirable behavior.

In most cases if you issue a correction, it should be seen out to its conclusion. But if there is legitimate reason to reverse that correction in the form of a relevant reward, then this can be appropriate in some - but not all - cases where it was you who issued the initial correction. If the correction was issued by another staff member, educator, parent or other authority figure, it's best to have an open discussion with them about your desire to reverse any correction they issued, lest you inadvertently step on someone's toes.

MATERIAL REWARD

I've heard negative talk from people before about using material rewards in behavior modification programs, with many of them saying that material rewards should not have any part in teaching kids to self-correct. However, this view just isn't realistic. The fact of the matter is that material rewards are as effective as any other type of reward, and in some cases even more so.

Even adults crave material rewards. In fact, most of what we do is reward-driven. From our paychecks to nights out on the town, expensive cars, extensive properties and homes, fancy toys and equipment, vacations and much more are all rewards for good behavior. This good behavior consists of regular contributions toward our careers, families and communities. So why wouldn't material rewards apply to children?

Material rewards should not generally be expected; meaning, don't carry candies in your pockets every day, passing them around freely. Instead, in order to make the material reward have the most impact, it should be known among the children you work with as a potential reward out of numerous possibilities; not a guaranteed one.

Of course, material rewards can be more than just candy. Money is a strong motivator for good behavior and is the reason why many parents pay their children a small "allowance." In fact, you can teach kids a great deal of the practical daily financial skills they will need in life by offering some type of monetary reward.

As an example, let's imagine that you have a child, Mikey, who is having trouble keeping his language in check and curses often. He can be allotted a certain allowance each week; let's say $10. But during the week, each time he curses, that allowance is reduced by one dollar. You can use this as a motivator all week long, and you can also use it as a redirection.

For instance, let's say that Mikey has lost $3 of his allowance so far for the week, but he's been making consistent efforts to curb his language. Then you recognize body language that indicates Mikey is getting agitated and may be about to curse. You can quickly redirect the situation by interjecting with a statement such as;

"Hey Mikey, you've been doing such a great job watching your language today that if you keep it up, I'm going to give you $2 of your allowance back."

In this case you've redirected potentially negative behavior and influenced future behavior with the offer of a delayed reward. If there are other children present, you've also established that good behavior has good results, and in some cases, those results can come in the form of cold hard cash.

You can also help children to make better decisions by giving them a choice of reward. Going back to Becky and Jessica again, if we are looking to reward Jessica in an effort to redirect Becky, we can give Jessica the option of choosing money or a candy bar, which assures us that both will find value in the interaction.

One of the reasons that money is a legitimate reward is because it can be used to purchase many different things. Whatever a child likes, they can try to save enough money to buy. This process teaches them how to manage money and gives them a better appreciation for the things that they buy with their own "hard-earned" money.

But this is not to say that sugar and cash is the only way to reward a child materially. Examples of some other excellent material rewards includes books, notebooks, special pens or pencils, art supplies, collectibles, phone or computer/tablet skins, etc.

I know of some homes for troubled kids that keep bowls of simple "prizes" on hand. These prizes include everything from gum and candy to sports cards and small dolls, rubber balls, stickers, dice, temporary tattoos, and much more. The prize bowls were an absolute hit among the kids at this house and served as powerful behavior motivators.

Ultimately, material rewards are not only acceptable, they are extremely effective. Just stop and think about your own life for a moment; how many material rewards do you hope for and seek out each day, each week, each month? When you examine your own behavior and what motivates you in this regard, it's easy to see that we are all motivated by material items, and there's nothing wrong with that.

Finally, we must remember that the composition of any reward isn't as important as its timeliness and relevance.

THEORETICAL REWARD

My editor, Russ Hudson, lived for 2 years at a home for troubled youth called Good-Will Hinckley. This home was a campus style group home and had been in operation for nearly 150 years. When Russ was there in the late 80's and early 90's, the institution operated on a point card system. In each home on the campus, a married couple and their assistant lived with and supervised up to 8 boys in a large home. When the boys (or girls, on the other side of the river that split the campus) did something "bad," they were assigned a certain amount of negative points. When they did something "good," they were assigned a certain number of positive points.

In order to obtain and/or keep privileges, the kids had to maintain a threshold of a certain daily, weekly, and monthly point goals. If at the end of the day their points didn't meet the daily threshold, then the next day there would be a loss of privileges, and similarly but on a higher scale at the weekly and monthly level.

This type of points system has been used by other institutions in the past and is no doubt in use today. This is part of what I classify as the Theoretical Reward system, where the system operates on intangible data that can later be used to "purchase" rewards like privileges.

Theoretical rewards can take a number of shapes, but one of my favorites is the sticker chart system. With this type of system, a chart is used to map the occurrence/s of negative and positive behaviors throughout the week. (This is especially effective as a type of social proof in a group setting) Certain highly visible stickers are used to indicate the type of behavior, so that the chart's overall results can be seen readily even at a distance.

At the end of a preset period - generally weekly but with difficult to manage kids, a daily period may be better - kids can total the number of positive stickers on their chart versus the number of negative stickers. The remaining balance will determine some or all of the following period's privileges, or in some cases a positive balance can be traded for a wide variety of material rewards.

It's easy to be creative with theoretical rewards, but the general model is the point system. According to Russ Hudson, this system was extremely effective at Good-Will Hinckley, and taught him how to be democratic and even-handed in his dealings with other people. For instance, the Hinckley program allowed kids who disagreed with an assessment of "negative points" to setup an appointment to plead their case in a very specific manner and within a specific time frame. This was called "Appropriately Disagreeing."

Children who earned enough positive points could be placed on a higher level of privileges called the Negotiation level, where at the end of each day and/or once per week, the children negotiated openly for their privileges for the following week, backing up their arguments with the previous period's point cards.

Other theoretical rewards include the awarding of intangible titles, characters or imaginary positions. For instance, in one small home for previously homeless youth, the kids and even the staff had become caught up in the Lord of the Rings frenzy. Staff of the home created a "fellowship" that split the kids into teams, with each team's members earning "rank" and/or special powers with their good behavior, and losing these items for their bad behavior. A chart was developed and at the end of the week the team with the highest score could take a vote to elect one of their members as Gandalf. This child then got to sit at the head of the table during meals for the next week in a funky-looking fake throne that one of the staff had picked up at a second hand store.

In this case, all of the rewards are theoretical. Earning rank and special powers, being elected as Gandalf; none of these are tangible rewards, but they work nonetheless. At the heart of this Lord of the Rings scheme is a point system, but with a little creativity; the staff of this home took things to a level that motivated the kids to want to behave well.

Additionally, the team environment taught the children to work together, and voting helped them to make democratic and diplomatic decisions that not all of them benefitted from directly. This meant that the children had to be courageous and selfless throughout the week, because they were dependent on votes from their peers to achieve the coveted position of Gandalf.

It all sounds a little dorky and it is; but that's what makes it great. This is just one example of how there are all sorts of different ways that you can reward children theoretically; and when done right it can be a lot of fun for both you and the kids.

PRIVILEGE REWARD

With today's technology-oriented kids, privileges are often more coveted than other types of rewards because they fill a social need that is strong in young people. For instance, telephone/cell phone usage, gaming, internet/social media use and the privilege of hanging out with friends are all potent motivators for good behavior. Offering these privileges as rewards can achieve incredible results among even the most unruly kids.

However, it's surprising how many traditional privileges can be offered as rewards. Time alone is a huge reward for some kids, and so is the privilege to go for a walk, hang out at the park, or have a friend over.

Unique privileges include offering a free pass from chores, sitting in a special chair or taking the "shotgun" seat when in the car, extra sleeping time in the morning, later bedtimes and more.

The great thing about extending a privilege as a reward is that you can choose a privilege-based reward that can be issued immediately, incrementally or delayed and still possesses relatively the same influence, depending on the reward and its relevancy to the behavior in question and the intended effect you wish it to have. This means that if you have a group of kids that are being rowdy, but one of them is behaving well, you can offer this child the reward of having some video game time alone in his room. Or, if you're trying to motivate the group to behave well, you can offer a group video game session on the condition of a set period of good behavior.

It's important to note that some privileges should not be restricted or used as a reward, and I can only caution you that you will have to recognize these cases when they arise. As an example, let's imagine that you work in an institutional setting with a traumatized young girl who takes special solace in chatting online with her best friend. During an especially difficult period in the girl's life, taking away this "privilege" could prove disastrous as this is a significant way for her to identify and address her feelings.

In order to recognize cases like these and for you to pinpoint privileges that should not be subject to reward or restriction efforts, you must know the children you work with, and you must be observant enough to know when they are experiencing a time of need that exempts certain privileges from being used as tools of behavior modification.

HONOR/AWARD

An honor or award can serve as a powerful and unique reward that most disadvantaged and troubled kids have little experience with. Certificates, awards and trophies, small ceremonies, large ceremonies, notes/cards of approval and appreciation are just a few of the ways that you can honor or award a child for a job well done. This is a powerful motivator for children because they crave recognition and want to be held in high regard by the people in their life. Honoring them and giving them awards is a tangible method of showing that indeed, you do hold them in high regard, and you think that other people should too.

But not every child wants to be rewarded in a way that brings social attention. Kids who are excessively shy, anxiety prone or those who suffer from severe cases of PTSD might not respond well to an honor or award that fixes attention on them. In these cases, finding a way to more discreetly honor the child is a wise approach, but is one that requires sharp observation skills and a genuine, even-handed presentation.

Honors and awards are effective rewards because they are extremely memorable, which instills long-term behavioral cues and reminders in children who are recipients. When other children are present, this type of reward also provides vital motivation to achieve similar standings as the peer being recognized, and can break the ground for an easier road to self-correction.

INCREASED RESPONSIBILITY

If we want children to be responsible, we must give them responsibilities. In some cases, these responsibilities can also be rewards. This is because children are not afraid of responsibilities when given the chance to rise up to them, and in the same way that telling students they are masters can cause them to become masters, we can help our children to be responsible by giving them responsibilities as part of a reward program.

For instance, let's imagine that you work in a state-run home for traumatized young girls. As part of a functioning household, the girls take turns with required assigned chores. One way to reward a specific girl who consistently does an excellent job with her chores is to assign her an additional duty as "chore checker." This reward is actually a responsibility that requires the girl to check the chores performed by each of the other girls for thoroughness.

However, this is also a position of trust and authority, and it shows that you recognize the girl's judgment as being sound. These are compliments of the highest order and often boost confidence in a way that will spur the child to want to achieve continued and additional success. The wanting or desire of these responsibilities that invariably comes is a sign of growth and maturity, and your granting of them is recognition of the same.

Other ways that you can promote responsibility by offering responsibilities as a reward include via special tasks and roles like that of flag bearer, mail checker, pet caretaker, person-in-charge situations, notes-taker, form collector, equipment operator (TV/DVD/Computer, etc.), menu planner, lawn mower duties (but usually only when it's a rider!), group moderator and many other responsibilities that lots of kids would be proud to take on.

Increased responsibilities are often coveted by children because they innately understand the message that it says to their peers;

I have been deemed competent and trustworthy in this task and as a result have gained a special skill, privilege, or both. I am a worthy example.

This type of reward is all about empowerment; we recognize one achievement or behavior by rewarding it with the immediate potential for an entirely new level of achievement, thereby empowering the child to better themselves.

Going back to my editor Russ Hudson, when he was at Good-Will Hinckley the highest level a child could achieve after the Negotiation level was the Achievement level. This level wasn't obtained through good behavior alone. It was obtained through legitimate "achievements" in the form of responsibilities handled well, and with it came a whole new frightening responsibility; freedom to self-regulate.

So you could say that offering responsibilities as rewards is representative of what Preemptive Behavior Therapy is all about; the path to self-correction.

SPECIAL EVENT

Special events allow us extreme flexibility in tailoring a reward to suit a specific child for specific accomplishments or behaviors. But using special events as a reward doesn't have to be reserved for those of us who work with groups of kids; it can just as easily be applied to situations where you only work with one child. Why not take a single child to the movies, or the park, or anywhere else, for that matter? Give them the opportunity to interact with other kids if they so choose, or take some time, just the two of you.

The options available to use special events as rewards are virtually endless, depending on your region and ability to come up with original ideas. In the past I have observed and participated in the following types of special events that were awarded as part of a behavior modification program;

Pizza parties, trips to the zoo, swimming and water games/sports, board game/trivia nights, karaoke, movies - both late night and matinees, hiking and camping trips, ice skating, sledding, shopping and trips to the mall, dress up games and parties and anything else you can think of will work, as long as it's relevant to the child or group you are rewarding.

Interestingly, I have found that the most rewarding special events are those that involve personal interactions with animals. When children interact (with positive guidance) with animals, it helps to relieve their anxieties, develop both sympathy and empathy, improve non-verbal communication skills and comprehension and overcome fears.

But more importantly, I have seen magic happen between troubled and high risk kids and animals. I've seen a puppy make a solemn little girl laugh, and I've seen a tough young man cry because of how much he loved a certain horse. I've seen violent kids become humane and compassionate, and I've seen withdrawn kids come out of their shells as a result of their work and interaction with animals.

Getting to know and care for any animal is a far different experience than interactions and relationships with other people. The fact of the matter is - and I don't need any studies or peer review to know this is true - that animals give us something that people cannot, and this something is a good thing. I believe that we need these types of experiences and interactions in order to become whole people, for until you look another creature in the eye and come to know them, you're missing an integral part of life here on this tiny blue planet.

Regardless of where you are, there exists abundant opportunities for you to introduce kids to animals. A local zoo is the most benign and removed type of experience, but you can also consider volunteer work on nearby farms or at your town's animal shelters or veterinary clinics. Horseback riding, dog and puppy training clinics, hatcheries, aviaries, bee colonies, chicken farms and more are all excellent ideas to get kids involved with animals.

Even if you have no funds available for this type of reward, in most cases that's not a problem. Many farms, sanctuaries, shelters, riding centers and other places involved in animal care will allow children to get involved at no cost. This can consist of grooming horses and shoveling stalls at a local equestrian center, or volunteering to walk dogs at a nearby shelter.

If you act intuitively and creatively, you are certain to come up with an animal-related reward system that can significantly impact a child's life forever.

CAUTION: Animals can be dangerous, even when it's not their intent to be dangerous. Proper knowledge and supervision is absolutely vital in order to assure a safe and practical experience.

PERSONAL COMMENDATION/PRAISE

Never underestimate the power of a simple "Thank you," or "I'm proud of you" as a reward. In fact, sometimes it is exactly this type of reward that a child wants; not a toy or money or candy or a trip to the park; just some praise and recognition from you.

Many troubled and high risk kids come from backgrounds where they were only recognized negatively. These kids crave the validation and social bonding that only direct rewards from your mouth can provide. Personal commendations, praise and encouragement as a type of reward are extremely effective when genuine and timely.

Don't forget that this type of personal reward can also consist of appropriate hugs, high-fives, thumbs-up, or just a clap on the back.

TIMING OF REWARDS

The timing of rewards should differ depending on what you hope to accomplish with the child. Like redirections and corrections, rewards can be instantaneous, delayed, incremental or sustained. In some cases, rewards may utilize two time frames. For instance, a reward where the first part of the reward occurs immediately, while a second part occurs in a delayed, incremental or sustained time frame.

For instance, using multiple time frames might come in handy in the case of Becky and Jessica mentioned earlier. Let's assume that Becky's bad behavior was mirrored by one or two other kids in your group, and Jessica was the only one who did not need to be redirected or corrected. So in the case mentioned earlier, the immediate part of the reward consists of a small candy bar given to Jessica, with the additional goal of redirecting Becky. But later, when things have quieted down and perhaps a change of staff has occurred, Jessica can be given a larger reward.

As an example, Jessica could be praised openly and awarded a gift certificate to her favorite clothing store. Or she could be granted special privileges like staying up extra late. However you choose to reward her, you've now added an additional time frame to the original reward, which was given for good behavior when other children were not behaving properly. Now, Jessica is getting recognition later on (which serves as yet another redirection for the others) and a supplement to the immediate reward that can be delayed, incremental, sustained or even just a second immediate reward.

This means that Jessica was rewarded during three different time frames:

1. Immediate reward of candy while rest of group was misbehaving
2. Delayed reward of praise and notification of larger reward

3. Application of larger reward

This also means that this one instance provides 3 unique opportunities to redirect the rest of the children.

The point is that if your reward issuance can serve multiple purposes, then you will be extremely effective as a credible authority figure in the lives of the children you work with.

REWARD COMMUNICATION

A reward should always be clearly communicated. This is especially true if you are using the reward for the dual purpose of validating one child's behavior while redirecting another's. It should be made clear to the child what they are being rewarded for, which will clearly outline what behaviors to avoid and what behaviors to engage in if they wish to receive an identical or similar reward in the future.

When I issue any type of reward - especially a material one - I always tell the child precisely what it's for:

"Jessica, you've really helped me today with your excellent behavior, so I want to reward you with this piece of candy."

"Mikey, you've been doing an amazing job using setting-appropriate language the last few days. I feel you deserve a reward, so I'm giving you back the few dollars you lost of your allowance earlier in the week."

This alleviates any chance of the illusion of favoritism, but it also clearly spells out your expectations for the future in a completely positive way.

Finally, I have witnessed how written statements of reward are exceptionally powerful. For instance, I have seen kids who, when awarded a certificate, written commendation or some other reward received in writing, will read and re-read the reward many, many times - even long after it has been presented. This is an extremely effective method of making the reward that you issue sustain itself for weeks and months to come while simultaneously motivating the child to make similar achievements.

Chapter Conclusion

We must remember that we are animals; this is a common theme throughout this book and with good reason. As animals, we have been built from the very beginning with powerful, lifelong reward systems in place that motivate and guide our behavior.

If we go about our days taking the rewards we earn like our income, homes, cars, toys, trips, etc., but we ignore the strong need for rewards in the children we work with, then we can only be referred to as hypocrites. Children need rewards. Whether it's something material or something immaterial doesn't matter as much as the act of recognition itself; if it's genuine and meaningful, you are going to have a positive impact in the life of that child.

Isn't that what we're all here for?

7 CLINICAL VS. HOME APPLICATION

For uniformity of practice, I would love to say that the principles of Preemptive Behavior Therapy can be applied universally regardless of the setting. Unfortunately, this is not the case. The difference between the clinical and at-home setting is striking, so of course there will be differences in application.

Interestingly, there is little to no difference between the application of Redirections and Corrections as defined by PBT. Both field professionals and at home caregivers will administer these foundational parts of the program in a similar manner:

*Body language will be controlled deliberately to send a specific message, or at the very least managed so as to not reveal an emotional state. Whether a parent or a professional, a calm and even-handed demeanor should be maintained during Redirections and Corrections.

*Redirections and Corrections administered will be devoid of emotional motivation. They must also be fair and relevant whether at home or in a clinical or professional setting.

*In any setting, the parent, guardian, teacher, staff member or counselor must know the child in order to properly redirect, correct and generally interact with them. While this is obviously more challenging for professionals, the requirement is still the same; trust and respect must be gained in order to make progress. Careful observation must take place in order to recognize Body Language Indicators and prepare and execute an effective Redirection.

The main similarity here is that all levels of caregivers must observe and exhibit the same basic behaviors. Both parents and social workers need to maintain their composure, and they both need to act fairly despite any perception of direct or indirect sleight or insult. This means that the real differences between professional and real world application of PBT is found in the Rewards.

THE DIFFERENCE IS IN THE REWARDS

The good news is that the differences are restricted to the Rewards part of the PBT program. The bad news is that there is an emotional component involved here that cannot be completely overcome.

For instance, after an outburst has been resolved, you can cradle and rock and hold your child and cry together if need be. But in the professional environment, this sort of behavior is off-limits. We must practice a policy of "friendly but never friends" in the clinical setting, and when physical-emotional contact occurs, we lose the ability to maintain this sometimes critically necessary function.

In simple language, rewards can be accompanied by or consist entirely of physical-emotional contact that can have lasting effects on a child's mental health. Clinicians and professionals are generally precluded from engaging in these types of behaviors. Consequently, those who work with troubled or traumatized kids in the professional setting must be more specific and relevant with the rewards that they issue, and seek to find other ways to reward at the emotional level.

But just because parents can be emotional with their children doesn't mean they have things easy or even that they have a leg-up over a professional. In fact this emotional benefit can sometimes cause significant problems when dealing with troubled kids.

THE CHALLENGE FOR PARENTS

The challenge for parents is primarily to ensure that they display the right balance of emotional rewards and affection while avoiding emotional manipulation at the hands of the child. Let's face it - many children will use their knowledge of your emotional attachment to them to their advantage, and manipulation of this type is something that parents must deal with far more often than those who work with children professionally.

But the real paradox here is that the emotional aspect of a parent or caregiver's relationship with their child can actually make PBT more challenging. One of the hardest things that at-home caregiver's struggle with is to not hold emotions and affection hostage as a result of negative behavior, redirections, corrections, etc. This can happen to a parent or guardian that has not found a method of separating their emotions out during interactions with the child. After repeated insults or atrocious behavior, a parent may naturally feel that withholding emotional involvement or affection is prudent and necessary, but in most cases it only further damages the relationship.

So the challenge for at-home caregivers is not being emotionally manipulated or emotionally manipulative. This is an extremely difficult balance to strike and in my opinion is the reason that many parents ultimately give up and seek professional help to manage their troubled, traumatized or high-risk children.

Study and application of the principles of Preemptive Behavior Therapy will go a long way toward managing challenging behaviors in kids and teens, but there's much more to it than that alone. You also need to learn to observe and manage yourself, and for most people this involves a great deal of retraining, which will be discussed in detail in Chapter 8.

THE CHALLENGE FOR PROFESSIONALS

In the clinical setting you must be friendly but never a friend. You must be an authority, but you must be reachable. Children must feel like you can be trusted, but trusted more to do what's right than to serve their purposes. This is a balancing act that even veteran professionals struggle with. In fact, I have often thought that this particular aspect of the job gets harder the longer I have done it.

At home a reward can be something as simple yet powerful as a hug. In a professional setting, this is often not an acceptable practice. Even when hugs are permitted by your company's regulations or bylines, they still tend to be more reserved than what a parent or at-home caregiver can legitimately provide. This is especially true of professional environments with multiple children present. Ultimately this means that in the professional setting, the most powerful types of rewards may not be possible.

This leaves professionals at a bit of a disadvantage when issuing rewards, but the severity of this handicap is dependent on a number of variables. The age of the child is one of the most important variables, as well as severity of previous abuse, neglect, family history, mental health, etc.

So how do you maintain professional boundaries while still getting close enough to know a child well and develop an individualized behavior modification plan?

BRIDGING THE GAP

For professionals, the emotional gap in the Reward component of PBT can be bridged by ensuring that there are emotional components to the rewards issued. In actuality this is a redundancy considering that the Reward section already clearly instructs that rewards should be as relevant as possible. Relevancy is determined in large part by potential or actual emotional investment (on the child's part) in the reward offered.

For instance, you can help a child acquire the emotional support and physical affection they need by arranging and/or helping to fund additional time with loved ones through visits, phone calls, texts/emails, letters, gift exchanges, etc. Barring this more direct approach, you can connect with a child emotionally by using what you know about them to select a particular reward that has emotional meaning to that child. If it's something that is unique to the child, you're probably on the right track.

Of course, it's important to point out that we should never punish by restricting access or reward by granting access to family or loved ones. The reward here is our additional efforts to take extraordinary measures to get them additional time or better quality time than customary. In this way, the reward is our intense interest and focus on getting them what they need and making certain that it is meaningful to them.

However, you don't have to think critically in this regard all the time. An enthusiastic "high-five" or a genuine handshake can take the place of a hug - especially if the child respects you. My editor claims that when he was a boy, a firm handshake with direct eye contact was one of the most powerful types of rewards he remembers. He lived in various group homes and shelters for troubled kids, so he has years of experience in this regard.

Of course, this all has to be genuine. If you're not being real with the kids you work with, they'll know it and so will you. This is probably the most challenging part of Rewards for practitioners of PBT in the professional setting, as it can take some time to generate a feeling of trust and respect sufficient enough that when you shake the child's hand for a job well done, they'll know you mean it, and therefore it will mean something to them. And there you have your emotional component: because you care about what the child cares about and reward them accordingly, that makes it emotional and suddenly you can bridge gaps that previously seemed impossible.

NO EASY COMPARISON

Are the principles of PBT easier to apply in the professional setting, or at home?

This is a question I get frequently and the only proper response is that one is not easier than the other. For instance, the emotional involvement of a parent can take its toll in the form of stress and worry. But working for years with troubled kids can be a heavy burden on a professional as well.

Of course, the rewards for both parents and professionals will ideally offset these stresses and burdens. After all, none of us who are professionals in the field chose to work with troubled kids in order to get rich financially, and parents have no choice in the matter. So it's clear that our motivations are to genuinely help these children.

The power of Preemptive Behavior Therapy is that it is based on animal models of behavior, which means that it predates organized society. Observing and working with kids at this level is completely different than the reactionary and corrective styles of parenting and behavior modification largely in use today. This makes it clear that regardless of the setting, the application is the same and so it cannot be said that being a parent is easier than being a professional when it comes to managing high-risk youth.

Most of the arguments that I hear about this topic are split into two general types, each arguing that the other role is more difficult:

*Parents argue that they have an advantage because they have a permanent emotional connection to their child.

*Professionals argue that they have an advantage because they have support and they get to go home at the end of the day.

Both are correct, but in the end it boils down to you and one child. It doesn't matter who you are, or where you are; it's natural, it's animalistic, and the principles are always the same: You observe the child. You learn their behaviors and body language. You redirect their behaviors when possible and correct them when necessary. You issue relevant rewards frequently. At the end of the day, we'll all go to sleep thinking about these kids - parents and professionals alike. It's not easy, but it is beautiful, and it works.

The only restrictions in the application of PBT are that professionals are restricted in the level of emotion they can put into rewards. These restrictions are meant to protect both children and professionals and are needed at least in part because we have not learned to build trust in each other in the right way. But by applying a framework like PBT unilaterally to the care of troubled and traumatized children, we can set expectations that can allow parents and professionals to work together.

After all, the primary objective for professionals is to (when possible and safe to do so) help a child work on their relationships with their families, with the eventual goal of reunification at whatever level is possible. This means that parents and professionals will often cross paths and need to work together. If both are applying the same sets of logical behavior conditioning principles, then the consistency this will bring to the child's life could significantly aid in the healing and behavioral improvement process.

Whether you are a parent or a professional, this is not easy work. But by operating within a framework like PBT, you can achieve significant success even with the most troubled and traumatized youth, and you can do so in a way that allows the child to correctly believe that they are self-correcting and managing their own behavior with you acting merely as a guide.

In my career I have worked with some children that other professionals had deemed hopeless. I've also worked with animals that various experts had deemed unreachable. I was able to bring these troubled souls - human and otherwise - back from the brink not through some complex new-fangled "system," but by simply observing them and reacting in the most natural way possible to what is indeed a natural environment.

When we see troubled kids, they are nothing more than animals lost in the forest, needing guidance. Sometimes these animals don't know that you're helping them and so you need to approach them with a specific protocol that is passive but determined, safe and logical. This very same system must also work when the animal - child - recognizes that you are trying to help them and resists.

This is why PBT can and should be adopted across the board.

8 RETRAINING YOU

The strangest part of this book is the fact that the Preemptive Behavior Therapy program does not actually begin until you have retrained yourself. So in reality this chapter should be "Chapter 1," but the necessity here to provide substantial background and foundational information in order to accomplish this retraining cannot be circumvented or accelerated.

You see, it's not enough to simply read this book and then begin to apply the principles within straight away. This is because most of PBT is based on body language and cues, but nearly everyone I have ever met uses, reads and interprets body language at a subconscious level most of the time. This is great because we as humans can understand each other through even the toughest spoken language barriers, but it's also a curse because most of us give away too much information with our body language.

This means that ultimately, you need to be retrained if you are to affect positive change in a child's life. This is not a manuscript that only teaches you to help children achieve self-correction - it is one that requires you to apply these same principles to yourself before you truly begin to apply them to others. In this regard, your work is just getting started, because you are also now on the path to self-correction, as you will see throughout this chapter.

Why is self-correction needed for adults, caregivers, clinicians and counselors?

Going back to the discussions of Chapter 2, we know that the old ways are dying and will no longer work for our purposes. One of the primary reasons why these old ways are dying is because we as adults and authority figures send mixed messages. We often say one thing, while our body language says something else entirely. We have lost touch with our natural state to the point that we no longer realize we have evolved to communicate and make powerful expressions with our bodies.

So out of our mouths come one thing and from our faces, hands and feet come other things. Children easily pick up on these contradictions; even if only subconsciously. But whether a child consciously or subconsciously recognizes contradictions in what you say and your body language, the general message is the same; you are not telling the whole truth.

Let's take a moment to clarify how this may have happened to you in the real world or the professional/clinical setting:

*Have you ever been frightened or concerned for your safety by a child or teenager when they were throwing a fit, behaving aggressively or otherwise acting dangerously?

*Have you ever had to dole out a consequence to a child that you just didn't want to enforce, but had to anyway?

*Have you ever been annoyed by a child who pestered, harried or harassed you or others incessantly?

*Has a child ever personally insulted you in a particularly nasty way?

 *Have you ever felt exasperation when dealing with a child who exhibited repetitive behavioral problems?

*Have you ever been emotionally touched by a child's vulnerability?

If you've experienced any of these things, chances are high that your body language was betraying you even if you think you held your emotions in check. The way you reveal your true emotions is probably not known to you at this moment and will require study and management, and that's what this chapter is all about.

Now, the idea that we should manage our natural body language is not an attempt to lie to the children, and in fact this is mostly impossible. After all, you will still feel the emotion, but you will be careful not to let your body language reveal it (unless appropriate) and will carry on acting professionally neutral. Feelings and emotions can be discussed when the interaction or event is under control in situations that call for it.

We must also remember that PBT is primarily designed for working with troubled, traumatized and high-risk children, which requires more restraint of emotions. Children who are emotionally healthy rarely respond in the same way as children who have been traumatized. This is not to say that PBT cannot work in a healthy home environment, but rather that the level of emotions and their corresponding displays of body language are different in each setting.

The chief point here is that your primary tool in this endeavor is the observation and interpretation of body language. Like a game of chess, a smart child can manipulate you if they figure out your natural-emotional Body Language Indicators - even in the professional or clinical setting. And if your body language opposes your words or other actions, then it's likely that the child will see you as being untruthful and your relationship with them will become far more challenging.

A CULTURAL PRACTICE

Another primary reason the old ways are dying is because we have become too far set in our ways of looking to correct a problem after it has already occurred instead of preventing the problem from ever happening in the first place. This is a cultural problem and can be easily observed as an example in the health care industry.

For instance, the vast majority of the population seeks treatment only when an injury or other condition occurs. Meanwhile, the professionals who work in the healthcare fields advise prevention over correction, while making a living mostly performing corrections. It's a conundrum of the worst sort.

Fortunately, the working principles of PBT correct this type of imbalance: we seek prevention over correction, but we correct only when we must and not as a modus operandi. In fact, just by the act of looking for BLI (body language indicators) that tell us some negative behavior might soon occur, we are straying from the traditional path of overseeing a child with our head cocked and brow raised, acting only when we need to issue a correction. In this model, we act beforehand. We act preemptively. In order to do so, we must break from our cultural programming via a curriculum of honest and only partially guided retraining.

RETRAINING GOALS

The overall retraining goals that you must achieve in order to successfully apply the principles of PBT can be summarized as follows:

1. *Prevention First*

This is comprised of learning how to observe and interpret the body language of the children you work with and using that knowledge to prevent negative thoughts from becoming negative actions.

2. *Manage Emotion-Induced Body Language*

You must observe and become vigilant in preemptively controlling your emotion-induced natural body language.

3. *Provide Emotionally-Based Rewards*

You must learn to create and administer rewards with emotional components.

While each of these goals is critical for all types of practitioners, some are more specifically geared toward one type of guardian. For instance, providing emotionally-based rewards is a more applicable and necessary goal for professionals because this group faces greater challenges in issuing these types of rewards. However, I have found that many parents and other at-home caregivers also struggle in this area after issuing rewards that have little relevance, no interaction and no long-term impact.

At the same time, it's probably fairly clear by now that parents, grandparents and other non-professionals taking care of high-risk kids specifically need to focus on managing emotion-induced body language. (I want to interject here for a minute and make one point about emotion-induced body language. Some would argue that *all* body language is emotion-induced, but they are only partially correct. The argument can actually be clarified as; all *natural* body language is emotion-induced, but not all body language is natural. For instance, consider that part of the PBT program for retraining yourself includes learning how to deliberately create body language positions and cues in order to elicit specific responses from the child you are interacting with. This body language is not natural; it is consciously manipulated, while in most cases natural body language is spurred unconsciously.) But I have witnessed plenty of clinicians, counselors, educators, behavioral technicians and other professionals exhibit obvious emotion-induced body language that contradicted what they were saying with words and gave away their true feelings. In most of these cases, the worker was not even aware that they had exhibited these BLI until it was later brought to their attention.

So these three goals for retraining are applicable to everyone who spends time with children in an authority position of any sort; be it as a parent, guidance counselor, social worker, legal guardian or anyone else. Thankfully, there are only 4 Steps that need to be taken in order to complete this part of the program, and they are all quite straight-forward.

STEP ONE: OBSERVING & RECORDING BODY LANGUAGE - OTHERS

The foundations of PBT are firmly rooted in the understanding of body language - our own, but even more importantly, that of the children we work with. The best way to understand both types of body language is to simply go out in the field and begin making observations and notations. But you don't have to be a field scientist or researcher in order to do so; the field is your home, school or workplace, and the observations are made in these natural environments without overly noticeable changes to your behavior.

Perhaps one of the best ways to start is by choosing one or two of the children you work with or parent for more specific observations. What I find is most efficient is to carry a very small notebook in my back pocket. I document body language indicators and notate their surroundings shortly after they occur. In general I tend to duck away in order to make my notes, as I have found it's best not to take notes in front of a subject, but if you don't subsequently get something written down your memory of the event will quickly fade and possibly become altered.

In order to simplify your observations, what you are primarily looking for is to notate moments of transition that involve you and the subject/s. Transitional moments are moments that cause a change in body language such as the following:

*Entering or exiting a room
*Engaging with a child
*Standing up & sitting down
*Making a direct query

*Changing physical position
*Issuing a redirection or correction
*Issuing a reward

Transitional moments are those that are most likely to elicit some type of body language response and therefore are the most logical places to start when observing and recording BLI. In fact, body language often signifies that something has changed emotionally within a person, so these transitional moments can occur as a result of an emotional trigger. Meaning, the transitional moment might happen after the emotion has already occurred, as opposed to the transitional moment triggering the body language reaction. There is a significant difference here but both can be observed and recorded in the same manner.

Whether body language is the result of a transition or an emotional response that causes a transition, there are certain things you should be looking for. During these moments, you'll want to take note of any changes in hand positioning - especially when the hands come up to touch or cover up the head or face.

You'll also want to look for leg, feet, and body "pointing," and pay special attention to the direction of the toes. Document everything that you can without causing changes in your own behavior. Some specific things you're looking for:

*Does the child meet or avert your gaze?
*Does the child change body position?
*Are the child's arms and legs open or closed?
*Is the general direction of the child's body language pointing toward or away from you?
*Do the same types of transitions lead to different body language, depending on the presence of others in the room?
*Are the hands tight, calm, or restless?
*Is the child exhibiting signs of mirroring you or someone else present?

These are just a few of the behavioral cues you should be expecting to observe. However, it's important that you remember that what you are looking for is animalistic body language. Dogs, horses, birds, ruminants, primates and many other animals all exhibit their own type of body language. We are essentially primates, which makes us no exception. This means that when you approach the observation of body language, you must remove yourself from the observation and view the behaviors of your subject as purely animalistic. This is 100% acceptable and healthy, and will not impede your ability to act professionally, because in Step Two you will be applying the same observation principles to yourself.

Observing, interpreting and recoding body language is a lot like learning multiple languages. Each language has fundamental principles and expressions that are trans-cultural in nature and can have the same exact meaning using different words/sounds. Body language in the animal kingdom is like this as well, meaning that most animals have ways of expressing the same or similar emotions. For instance, whether the subject in question is a horse, a cat, a dolphin or a gorilla, they all express frustration with body language. They all express grief, elation, loneliness, playfulness and excitement; but they all do it just a little bit differently. Nevertheless, these are animal languages that can be learned.

Most humans pay very little conscious attention to body language, so they don't really know what to look for other than the obvious cues when they start to study the body language of their peers or children. Even though the body language is something that we produce, we know very little of it, which means that we require careful study in this regard.

As an example, imagine that you are about to begin working with horses, but have never worked with them before and have no formal education about the animals. In your case, you wouldn't understand what different ear positions mean. You'd be oblivious to the meaning of head positioning. You probably would understand obvious behaviors like charging and stamping, but you might not recognize when these behaviors are actually invitations to play.

You would need to spend time with horses, observing them in all of their different states in order to begin to understand what they are saying when they speak in body language.

Likewise, you'll need to study humans as well. We rely so much on verbal communication that we rarely know anything about our own body language. You need to stand outside the fence and observe, and you need to seek out the counsel of those who have already done so.

Because I know that it can be hard to stay organized in our chaotic modern lives, I'm going to create a transitional BLI tracking sheet for you within these pages so that you can keep at least your initial observations and notations in one centralized place for quick reference. I have filled in the first few lines with some mock information:

SUBJECT	DATE	TRANSITION TYPE | TRIGGER	RESULTANT BODY LANGUAGE
DCH	01/03/14	Entered room	Shifted - knees & feet pointed away
DCH	01/03/14	Direct engage	Hand to forehead, over eyes
RJB	01/04/14	Sat down	Mirrored me, 2 positions

Preemptive Behavior Therapy

SUBJECT	DATE	TRANSITION TYPE | TRIGGER	RESULTANT BODY LANGUAGE

You should plan on spending at least 2 weeks observing the body language of the children you interact with in the course of a day. The more time you spend doing this, the quicker you will begin to see behavior patterns related to the body language you are observing.

This information is the diamond in the rough that we are attempting to get to; by analyzing these patterns, you will be able to develop a schematic of what specific body language means in a specific child. This sets the stage for you to redirect the child instead of correcting them, because you will be able to accurately predict impending behaviors based on the precipitating BLI.

When you step back and review your notes after a period of weeks, you may realize that the child or children you work with are trying to tell you something that you didn't notice before. With consistency in observation you will become an extremely effective parent or caregiver because you will immediately recognize deviations from the normal behavioral patterns you have witnessed and notated.

After careful observation and interpretation of the body language of any individual, you will find yourself recognizing nuanced BLI that before was not distinguishable to you at all. You will likely begin to pick up on highly individualized BLI variations that cannot be accurately described by texts. This is because over time, the fact that you are consciously studying body language leads to your subconscious' ability to pick up and interpret BLI becoming stronger.

I believe that regardless of how sharply we observe body language and how carefully we control our own; there will always be the conscious and separate subconscious recognition and expression of body language among humans. This is especially true the moment we open our mouths, which instantly devotes most of our brain's focus on what we are saying, while the natural, subconscious communication of body language continues unabated and largely without our recognition of it.

Because so much of human expression is wrapped up in our uncontrolled emotions, being masterful when it comes to body language can do vastly more for you than just help you work with a troubled or traumatized child. It can help you communicate and understand people everywhere on an entirely new level that opens previously closed doors and paths.

But perhaps more importantly - certainly for our purposes at least - being adept at rapidly recognizing and assessing patterns of body language can help you help others. Ultimately, that's why this is the first actionable step you will take as part of the PBT program.

STEP TWO: CONTROLLING IMPULSIVE EMOTIONAL BODY LANGUAGE - SELF

Recognizing and managing your body language is essential in order to remain calmly impartial during interactions with children that cause natural emotional reactions. Often this is not easy. After all, we are all human and we respond to the same types of events and behaviors in similar ways. We feel, we hurt, we hope, we succeed and we have many different ways of expressing these and other emotions and concepts. This can make it extremely challenging to remain even-handed and calm during a difficult exchange with a misbehaving child.

But more importantly, we often lie to children, and our body language gives us away. How many times have you brushed aside questions such as *"Are you mad at me?"* with a dismissive "*No…*" The fact of the matter is that the child is picking up on your body language, which tells them that you are angry or frustrated. It is your body language that caused the child to ask the question in the first place, so innately and subconsciously they already know the answer. But if you contradict your body language and tell them you are not angry, you are for all intents and purposes lying.

Therefore, it's best to learn to control your body language. This is not an attempt to break you of emotion; rather it is to teach you how to control those emotions for the benefit of another person. If a child can sense through your body language that you are upset emotionally, then their level of upset will be increased and feed on your own. Because you are in the position of authority and you must act fairly, it is your responsibility to control yourself to a higher degree.

One of the most efficient ways of learning to recognize and manage your own body language is to observe yourself in the field for a minimum of two weeks. At this moment you might think that you are excellent at controlling your emotional responses and body language, but chances are that you have dozens of "tells" or reveals that disclose how you feel during emotional interactions - you're just not conscious of them yet.

The second actionable step in Preemptive Behavior Therapy is to consistently observe, record and analyze your own body language during transitional and emotional events. You will quickly find that this is difficult to do and will require your complete focus in order to achieve any level of success. This is because concentrating on observing and controlling your own body language becomes quite hard while you are talking or otherwise in the middle of a direct interaction with a child. So the first step is to program yourself to observe YOU, and that's going to take some practice.

The following tracking sheet should be used in very much the same way as the tracking sheet for Step One. Your task is to take notice of your body language during transitional events such as entering or exiting a room, engaging in a conversation, sitting down or standing up, etc. You should pay special attention to any body language - however slight - during verbal exchanges with the children you care for as well as the adults that cross paths with you in an average day.

For 3 weeks you should use the following tracking sheet to observe and record the body language that you exhibit each day. The hardest part will be remembering to observe yourself. Most of us are so inwardly focused that it is difficult to attempt to see ourselves from the outside, and this is the real exercise here. What body language are you portraying to the world, when are you doing it and what does it mean? That is the point of this next exercise, with a few initial examples to give you an idea of how to get started:

DATE	EMOTION OR TRANSITION EVENT	RESULTANT BODY LANGUAGE
01/06/2014	RJB called me a "fat f'in bitch"	Hand clenched and covered mouth
01/06/2014	Direct correction of RJB	Arms crossed defensively
01/07/2014	Staff PKR entered room	Pointing behavior - knees and feet at PKR
01/07/2014	Engaged conversation with PKR	Mirror behavior - 1 position, legs crossed, arms down

Preemptive Behavior Therapy

DATE	EMOTION OR TRANSITION EVENT	RESULTANT BODY LANGUAGE

DATE	EMOTION OR TRANSITION EVENT	RESULTANT BODY LANGUAGE

At the end of each week you should go back and spend some time analyzing the data collected on this sheet. You can also analyze the data at the end of each day in order to see things with a fresh mind. Using the sheet, reexamine each event and try to remember what you were feeling at the time. What precisely was the specific emotion or feeling that caused you to exhibit a specific set of BLI? Did you realize the body language while it was happening or after it had already occurred? How did the event or episode in question turn out - negative, positive or neutral?

It may be wise to create additional spreadsheets to collect and analyze these thoughts, but at the very least you should be looking at your BLI tracking sheet once per week and asking yourself these extremely pertinent questions.

As your own body language patterns emerge, you will begin to see certain types of situations that cause specific related body language in you. These patterns are an excellent place to begin working on improving your ability to manage your body language, as they provide a consistent base from which to operate. Once you are familiar with your own BLI patterns, you can begin to formulate ways of arresting your normal impulses to exhibit certain BLI and learn to gain control over your body and facial expressions.

Natural body language impulses are exceptionally strong and difficult to predict and control. This means that developing the ability to recognize when an emotion-induced BLI is about to occur and arresting or modifying that behavior before it happens will likely be one of the most challenging of the tasks before you. Fortunately, there are a few effective techniques that you can learn for this purpose.

STALL & REDIRECT TECHNIQUE

The Stall and Redirect technique is based on one short statement designed to stall the forward momentum of the current conversation or interaction, and then a follow-up statement that redirects it. This technique always includes a precursor statement that permits you to break the moment. This precursor statement acknowledges the child or individual and deliberately plants the suggestion to begin redirecting the conversation:

"Betty, let's take a look at this together from a different angle, okay?"
"Michael, let the two of us see if there is a better way to approach this whole thing."
"I think we should look at this in a new light - can I ask you something?"
"You may be right in some ways, but have you considered the following..."

These types of statements can be interjected any time the interaction is causing you to feel emotional about the situation. Statements like these essentially break the moment and allow a short reprieve in intensity. This is the Stall part of this technique, and will provide you with the time needed to manage your body language and begin to redirect the interaction.

This precursor statement should be immediately followed by your attempt to reframe the situation. This will consist of you offering some new unique way of looking at things. It's a useful exercise for the child, and it continues to allow you to maintain control over your body language. So in the above cases, we can imagine that the Stall and Redirect technique will look something like this:

STALL >>> "Betty, let's take a look at this together from a different angle, okay?" {here you have taken a moment to control your BLI} REDIRECT >>> "When you cuss at people, it makes others think that you're not very smart. That's not really fair to you because you are extremely intelligent."

STALL >>> "Michael, let the two of us see if there is a better way to approach this whole thing." REDIRECT >>> If you sign an agreement stating that you'll follow through on your responsibilities for the rest of the week, I'll let you go on that special outing tomorrow. But if you default on that promise, then your privileges will be restricted for two additional weeks.

STALL >>> "I think we should look at this in a new light - can I ask you something?" REDIRECT >>>
"What specifically would make you happy right now, and how are you willing to compromise in order to make that happen?"

The Stall & Redirect technique works by arresting the conversation flow, creating a new setting and making it easier to leave other parts of the conversation or actions behind. It also allows you time to conceal and recover in the event that you feel your body language, facial expressions, etc. will reveal your emotional state.

Despite its effectiveness, this technique can be misapplied if your particular method appears as disinterest. For instance, stalling by looking at your watch, checking your phone or changing position in a way that puts your back to the child can make it seem that you've lost interest or given up on the interaction. This means that your Stalling efforts must be arresting but genuine and pointed; you must make a definitive statement that halts the current interaction. You must then follow up with a legitimate query designed to place the ball back in the child's court and give them a feeling of control over the situation.

THE TRANSITION TECHNIQUE

The Transition Technique relies on shifts in thought processes and emotions in order to allow you time to control your emotions or regain your composure. These shifts consist of physical movements designed to act as a brake on the current interaction or engagement and create a moment of redirection.

The transition in question must be significant enough to create a shift in consciousness in both you and the child or young adult you are working with. It cannot be something as slight and simple as a change in hand position or shifting from open to crossed legs. Instead, the transition should be obvious and confident without being dismissive or flippant.

For instance, my favorite way of applying the transition technique is to stand up if I am sitting down, or to sit down if I am standing up. When I stand up I also generally back away a few steps in order to give the child space and freedom to think, recover and control their own emotions. These physical movements help to break the flow of the current interaction and allow me time to control my body language and plan what I might say or do next.

You can also arrest the current direction of an interaction by remaining seated or standing, but you must significantly alter your position. In particular, this means that you should change at least 2 major body positions, for instance, the legs and head, arms and waist, pointing knees and feet, arms and legs, hands and facial expression, etc.

The physical transition must be followed by a shift in the conversation in the same style as outlined for the Stall and Redirect technique. This is because any time you have successfully "stalled" the interaction, you have effectively created a Flicker moment. When working with horses we know that when the Flicker is achieved, you have gained a momentary window of focus from the animal. There must follow an instruction, request or command.

The same is true whether you use the Stall & Redirect or the Transition Technique. Either technique gives you valuable time to manage your own body language, but it also provides you with an opportunity to capture a Flicker moment and issue a redirection. However, it's important to keep in mind that the redirection isn't always focused on the child - it can be interaction-specific - meaning; it's not the child's behavior or thought processes that need to be redirected, but rather the interaction itself or your reaction to it.

Interestingly, changes in position often indicate changes in thought pattern, mood or attitude. So while you as a parent or professional might change your position in order to manage your own body language and control an interaction, you should also take notice when a child changes position during a conversation or engagement of any type. In some cases this repositioning could be natural, but in many cases it indicates a shift in consciousness that you should pay close attention to.

THE TRUTH TECHNIQUE

Ultimately, it may be best to actually come right out and tell a child how you are feeling if you are not able to control your body language. This is especially true for parents and other at-home caregivers who have more flexibility in the level of emotion expressed in any particular interaction. Honesty can sometimes be the best policy, but when working with troubled and high risk kids this is not always the case. Therefore, a calm demeanor with carefully controlled body language is ideal.

The Truth Technique involves carefully explaining your feelings to a child and planting the "suggestion" of a redirection. For instance, let's imagine that a child has just cussed you out. Your natural reaction is anger and you feel more than a little insulted, but this is not what you want to display with your body language. But you don't have to make a bodily display of your feelings; you can come right out and diplomatically state them instead, which generally serves to arrest the forward motion of the interaction:

"Because I care about your future, the fact that I am not reaching you is frustrating me right now and I'd like you to help me get this figured out."

"I think you are intelligent and so your opinion matters to me, which is why it's insulting when you curse at me and it makes me less willing to give you leeway."

"Your ability to hurt me only indicates how much I care about you."

"I can't help you if you're trying to hurt me."

"This conversation is making me angry, so I'm going to step into the other room for a few minutes."

Despite the fact that this technique requires you to come right out and state what you are feeling, it's vital that you remember that the actual presentation of these feelings should be in a non-emotional or heated way. You must still remain cool and collected. The point of telling the truth is to allow you the time to breathe and maintain your ability to manage your body language. Explaining carefully to a child that you are upset by their behavior is a lot different than not explaining and instead having your feelings be known by body language.

You may develop or already use techniques to control your body language that are not discussed here, or that are a hybrid of what's discussed here. Regardless of what specific techniques you use, you likely won't have much success without proper study of the body language of the children you work with and the body language that you display. Fortunately, over time your reliance on these techniques will decrease as your consciousness regarding your body language becomes more refined and practiced. This means that you should constantly practice a policy of observation and analysis as laid out here in the PBT manual.

STEP THREE: USING DELIBERATE BODY LANGUAGE TO DIRECT INTERACTIONS

Successful public speakers, politicians, businesspeople and world leaders often deliberately and effectively manipulate their body language to achieve a desired effect. In fact, many of them have trained extensively or have been coached professionally on how to do this, and there are a number of techniques that, if the industry had its way, would remain secret.

The power of using body language to deliberately manipulate an individual or a crowd is extremely potent and effective. People who use body language to create a specific feeling, state of compliance or to direct and keep an interaction flowing to their advantage know that a sweep of the arm can sometimes be more powerful than any words. They understand that the direction of their feet and legs tells their listeners where they want to go.

Successful people use this body language knowledge to their benefit because they know that long after people have stopped listening to them (listening - truly listening - is difficult for human beings) their subconscious will be closely following the speaker's body language. Ultimately, it is the cues that we receive subconsciously that are the most lasting and impactful, and there are well-trained individuals out there who know how to capitalize on this.

Professionals, parents and caregivers can also learn how to use their body language to achieve certain effects. The fact of the matter is that you don't just have to manage your own body language in order to mask emotion. Instead you can take a much more proactive role by deliberately positioning your body language to send a specific message, to reinforce what you're currently saying, to invite further discussion, or even to discourage behaviors or conversation flows/directions.

However, you don't have to look to high-profile individuals to see how body language can be used to guide interactions. You can find this powerful skill being wielded on farms, racetracks, training centers and nearly everywhere that people are working with dogs or horses. This also applies to work with other less common animals like dolphins, apes and birds, but my experience is with canines and equines. When working in these fields you learn the power of body language quickly because dogs and horses can't vocalize the full range of emotions that humans can. In fact, they are much more reliant on body language communication than on vocalizations.

Animals use body language to exert influence over their counterparts. In the canine world, we see that merely the way the teeth are exposed can express anything from fear to aggression to playfulness to submission. Depending on the position of the animal in the group, this can cause others to act in highly specific ways.

When a top-level trainer works with a horse in the ring, you often won't hear anything except the soft thud of hoof beats. That's because trainers operate primarily via body language, using certain physical signals instead of vocalizations to ask their horse to perform specific tasks. While these signals are learned by the horse through repetition training, the reason that they work is because of the innate level at which animals understand and respond to body language.

Even without intending to, our body language can move animals to take certain actions. For instance, after the passing of one of her family members, a friend was standing at the fence watching her horses playing around in the paddock. Her mind eventually drifted and she recalled feeling sad and melancholy; she sighed and put her head in her arms and rested on the top post.

One of her horses stopped its play and slowly walked over to her. He gently laid his head on her shoulder. He did not finish chewing the hay in his mouth or shift his feet; he stood still and just comforted her. The only logical theory here is that he picked up on my friend's body language and was compelled to go to her.

Another example is any child that has ever triggered a chase or attack by running away in fear from a dog. Although the child doesn't know it, their facial expression of fear and the act of running tells the dog that the child is prey. In these cases, sometimes even good dogs get confused.

In the case of a dog attack above, in theory the child violated some cardinal rules; he probably gave direct eye contact, his eyes undoubtedly widened the moment he felt fear, and he ran from a predatory animal. This is indicative of the idea of universal body language - that is, body language that can be understood cross-species.

For instance, imagine a pack of wolves in Siberia that has never encountered man before. If one or two of the wolves did encounter a man, and the man stomped his feet, beat his chest, huffed and puffed and growled; if he glared at the wolves, bared his teeth and squared off against them, the wolves would probably back off or retreat. This is even more likely if the man was sizable enough to give even more credence to his aggressive behavior.

The point here is that the wolves would understand precisely what the man was communicating, even though he did not use any words. The wolves innately understood the body language, and the man innately knew that the wolves would get his point.

Universal body language - eye contact, teeth baring, feet stamping, squaring off, glaring, etc., indicates that using body language to influence or direct other animals and individual animals within a species is an ancient evolutionary tactic. But because we have developed complex spoken languages, humans almost categorically do not deliberately manage, control or use their own body language consciously. We feel that we communicate best with words, but we are grossly mistaken.

If we look carefully we can easily see that body language is the most significant method of communication among all animals. And are we not animals as well? Can we not wield influence via body language? The answer is that we absolutely can. The following are a number of ways that home-based caregivers and professionals can use body language with children and teens (and adults too!) to elicit a desired effect. This is based on my professional experience working with children and animals. It has been adapted for PBT specifically for use with troubled, traumatized and high risk kids, but will likely work with anyone.

Open Arms - In my experience leaving your arms open indicates that you are "open" to discussion, negotiation, or that you are "open" to the ideas, feelings or concepts being discussed. However, open arms doesn't mean open and wide - open and wide signals dominance and/or indifference. Instead, your arms should be open at about shoulder width. If seated they can be at your side or in your lap; if standing clasped hands in front is okay but ideally your arms should be down - signifying that you have no "attack" in mind.

Opening your arms can be done in conjunction with or as an independent transition. For instance, if your arms are crossed to indicate displeasure with a badly misbehaving child, you can uncross them when the child begins to calm, signifying that calmness will make you more pliable - even if this is not actually the case.

Crossed Arms - Obviously the opposite of open arms, this is a negative stance and should only be used deliberately when necessary. Crossed arms act as a barrier to you - they tell your audience that you are not open to what they are saying or doing. This is an effective body language technique to use in situations where bad behavior is escalating.

There are a couple of levels of the crossed arms posture. Crossed arms with open legs send the message that while you are not exactly pleased at the moment, you might be ready to be convinced or concede; you are starting to become pliable. Conversely, crossed arms and crossed legs indicate resistance, disbelief or extreme displeasure. It is also an excellent position to take when a tirade has been launched against you, as it makes you appear well-fortified and impervious to attack.

Fingers Interlaced, Leaning on Knees While Sitting - With your elbows on your legs, leaning forward with your fingers interlaced in front of you is one of the most effective techniques I have found for using body language to reach kids - especially in situations where they have shut down. As you lean in to this position, you are literally pointing your entire body at the child, sending a clear signal that they have your full attention. It also tells them that you want to hear what they have to say, and that you want to be closer to them. These are potent messages.

Interlaced fingers tells your audience that while you are leaning in to hear them, you are still reserved until they meet you some of the way in this interaction. Once the child moves in a positive direction, the fingers can be unlaced and the arms opened, allowing the positive flow of interactions to continue.

Glace at Watch - Another type of negative body language, this should not be a regular practice. However, in some cases glancing at your watch or a clock can be extremely effective. This behavior sends a heavily laden message without using any words at all and can be done even while the subject is in the middle of an outburst. Glancing at your watch indicates that your patience is finite, and that a "deadline" will soon be reached where consequences may be ratcheted up. This body language should be reserved for after a correction has already been issued, but highly proficient practitioners of PBT may find it effective if used subtly as a redirection. However, it should be noted that as a "negative" body language, this should not be a customary redirection technique.

Nodding - By nodding affirmatively, you can silently encourage a child to continue and possibly expand upon their current behavior, conversation thread or interaction. At the very least it tells the child that you are listening to them and understand what they are saying. It doesn't signify that you agree with the child; only that you comprehend them and have heard them out.

Pointed Feet & Legs - This technique of using body language to influence behavior makes use of the feet and legs to "point" to what or whom you feel is important at the moment. For instance, imagine that you are in a group setting and there is one adult in particular speaking to several children. However, some of the children are not listening very well. By pointing your feet and knees in the direction of the speaker, your body language tells viewers that you believe this person should be listened to, or that you are supportive of or want to give credence to the specifics of what they are saying.

You can also use this technique on an individual, one-on-one basis. By pointing your feet and knees at the child, you are telling them that the only "direction" you are going in is theirs. It shows that you are listening and interested, and depending on how you hold your arms, indicates that you are receptive to their ideas, emotions, statements or behavior.

Mirroring - Usually when mirroring occurs naturally, neither party notices it even though the message is clear. Therefore, if you deliberately mirror someone else, they are not likely to become aware of it...consciously. But they will be aware of it subconsciously, and this can significantly aid your position. That's because mirroring means "I like you," "we are a team," or "I am comfortable with you."

Mirroring should only occur with natural body language, and unless you're looking for a fight, it should only be used with positive body language. Meaning, if the kid you are trying to talk to has her arms and legs crossed, you would not be wise to mirror her. Instead, mirror only neutral or positive body language.

If a child changes position frequently during an interaction, don't try to mirror most or all of their positions. Instead, one of the most effective practices is to start mirroring during a transition; when one of you changes physical position, when a major shift in the conversation has occurred, or when someone has entered or left the room. This way your deliberate attempt at mirroring will be masked by a natural transition that will help to reinforce your new position.

Smiling - Sorely underestimated and underused, even if you don't feel like something is funny or particularly happy, a smile will go a long way with almost any child or adult. You can use a smile to reinforce an idea, to signify agreement, to express solidarity or support and much more. The smile is a valuable and underutilized tool, and few outside of those who are trained to do so smile by deliberate conscious act in order to elicit a certain impression or to influence the actions or behavior of another individual.

A smile is especially useful as a tool to disarm or defuse a situation, or to indicate that despite negativity occurring at the moment, there is hope for change soon. A smile is one of the easiest and fastest ways to learn how to use your body language to influence those around you.

The preceding are my favorite ways of using my body language to help guide interactions and behaviors, but there are many other ways of doing so using various body language types and patterns. You might have something that works well for you, or you might find something effective in Chapter 9's resource section. There is no right or wrong answer here, but I can confirm that these methods are - for me, in a professional capacity - the most easily learned and readily applied methods of using conscious and planned body language to direct interactions.

STEP FOUR: REWARD BRAINSTORMING

The final major step in retraining yourself is to ensure that there are emotional components to rewards that you issue a moderate percentage of the time. Some rewards can be arbitrary and "petty" or simply for fun, but every so often you need to make sure that you are rewarding children in ways that are important to them. This is especially true for people in professional fields who cannot share the same level of emotional involvement that parents and other close guardians can.

I look at this a little bit like I look at Christmas lists. I rarely get or pay much attention to these lists. Instead I get out my notebook and think about the person I'm giving a gift to. I jot down notes of the most important things that I know about them, memories that I share with them, and whatever other details I can think of that will help me choose a meaningful gift for them.

Reward Brainstorming is basically like this. In order to generate a reward plan for a child, you must first observe them according to the PBT protocols and document and analyze their body language and behaviors. This will provide you with a wealth of information from which to operate. The general idea is to brainstorm certain aspects of a child's interests, personality, history and accomplishments in order to generate ideas for rewards that have significant meaning and lasting impact.

As an example, if we reward a child with a lollipop for good behavior today, they'll enjoy it once and toss the wrapper in the trash. But if we reward a child with a special trip to the local zoo to see their favorite animal - canis lupus - then we have helped to create a memory for life that will continue to drive behavior later on. Think about it for a moment - if you are using rewards partly as motivators for future behavior, which of these rewards do you think will have a longer lasting effect - the lollipop or the wolves?

At this stage of the PBT program you will have observed the body language and behaviors of the child in question extensively. You now have some important knowledge about him or her after analyzing your tracking sheet data, and based on your actual experiences with the child. You will now use this knowledge to brainstorm a list of potential rewards with emotional components. I have created a template style list to get you started, but keep in mind that this is a brainstorming list only. The rows are not necessarily related - they are grouped this way to help you easily pinpoint where groups of data indicate a trend that can be entered as a potential reward idea. As you start to fill out a row from left to right, you will likely find that each row or column spawns another idea that is often closely related:

Likes - Toys N Things	Important People	Favorite Places	Significant Needs	What is Reward for?	Reward Ideas
My Little Pony	Mother	Green fields	New boots	Helping another kid when sad	Couple hours at local riding center with mum
Mystery books	Grammie	Mitchell Pond			Write or call Grammie & ask to send new books, fund half
Lacrosse	Local teacher	Al's Cheeseburgers	New notebooks for school	Excellent grades	Cheeseburger at local game with teacher, announced inside new notebook!
Computer games		Bedroom when no roommate	Alone time	Well done chores	$5 game card and free time in room
Mobile phone	Indigo Girls	Home Ec. Class		Obeying phone use rules	New IG ring tone

Preemptive Behavior Therapy

Likes - Toys N Things	Important People	Favorite Places	Significant Needs	What is Reward for?	Reward Ideas

When you brainstorm at this level you will suddenly begin to see rewards in an entirely new way. Instead of arbitrary, impersonal and short-lasting rewards, we can instead easily develop meaningful, emotional and long-lasting rewards that will keep working for us - and the children - for months and perhaps years to come. It usually doesn't require much or any money at all, and in most cases you can devise rewards that can be applied right at home. The point is to make the reward mean something to the child if you want the lesson to be retained. Brainstorming everything you could reasonably know about the child is an effective way of achieving this goal

Chapter Conclusion

To recap, the first actionable part of the Preemptive Behavior Therapy program is to retrain YOU. This includes 4 major steps in the following order:

Step 1: Observe & Record Body Language - Subjects
Step 2: Control Impulsive Emotional Body Language - Self
Step 3: Use Deliberate Body Language to Direct Interactions
Step 4: Reward Brainstorming

You are prepared to take these steps and begin the PBT program because you are familiar with its foundations and you realize why the old ways are dying. You are able to recognize body language and understand what it means. You know the principles of the Flicker theory and its relation to BLI. You know how to issue an effective redirection, and you're competent enough to issue a correction when this isn't enough. You know how to create meaningful and impactful rewards and your new views on body language are changing the way you approach the world.

You're ready to make a difference.

9 CONCLUSION & RESOURCES

Preemptive Behavior Therapy might be a natural program, but it doesn't "come naturally." The most challenging part of PBT is not the actual learning of the concepts and how to apply them - instead, the challenge is found in *consistent* application. Often people have epiphanies and become excited about a new idea, practice or concept, but then they only apply it for a short while before going back to their old ways. Later they wonder why they were unsuccessful in their endeavors, when the sole reason is that they just didn't practice consistently.

The framework of Preemptive Behavior Therapy is like most other concepts that represent a better way of doing things than those that came before them; in time and with enough practice, it's hard to imagine going back to the old inefficient, antiquated ways. But you have to reach that tipping point first, and that requires a considerable amount of retraining and practice.

Nevertheless, it's important to keep in mind that the old maxim "practice makes perfect" just isn't accurate as that is impossible; we can perfect almost nothing in life, and certainly not our interactions with other humans over whom we largely have no control. There are always ways to improve. Instead, a better maxim might be; "Practice makes Proficient." Once you are proficient, constant practice will keep you proficient, and passion for the challenge will morph your proficiency into a higher level of performance and success over time.

One fundamental aspect of practicing takes things beyond the actual application of a new principle, idea, concept or process. This is to create an environment that supports, stimulates and supplements the efforts you are putting forth. For instance, writing down your daily goals before you start each day can help you focus your application of a concept or system later in the day, but it sets the frame for you to enter this mindset before you actually begin your day. A weekly writing session on the weekends can be helpful in making your daily progress easily visible and provide you with motivation to keep practicing even when you are at home relaxing.

Other people write these goals in lipstick or erasable marker on whiteboards or mirrors each day. Some send them from their home computer or phone to their own email inbox at work so when they arrive and login they will be reminded of their goals. The idea is to plant reminders in places where they will be well-received. This way, you will always be "thinking" about the concepts and ideas, even if subconsciously.

Returning frequently to your training materials is also part of practice and can be done at any time. You can review this book or any of the resources mentioned in this chapter, or you can print other helpful materials and post them in conspicuous places.

For instance, notes that you have taken or training materials that have been provided to you can be posted in any location where you need reminders and visible cues to keep practicing. Eventually these will begin to serve as subconscious guides to continually keep the idea of these new concepts fresh and to keep you motivated to practice enough to find yourself becoming proficient and preferring these news ways over the old.

To this end I have created the Preemptive Behavior Therapy program *At-a-Glance* sheet found on the following page. This sheet summarizes all of the key concepts of PBT and lists critical points of their application and practice. The graphic also lists the core philosophies of the program and the main running tasks that you must adhere to in order to achieve the highest levels of success with PBT.

I recommend printing this graphic and posting it in a place that you frequent often throughout the day. This could be at home or work, or both; depending on your particular situation. However, in order to use the sheet effectively, your first goal will be to study this manual enough so that the terms on the At-a-Glance are immediately familiar to you and so that you know automatically what each short point entails.

Feel free to print and unreservedly use this sheet, or make derivations of it if you prefer a different style or want to summarize even further. You can find the sheet on the PBT website, www.preemptive.info

Preemptive Behavior Therapy
At - A - Glance

1. OBSERVE BLI/FLICKER

BLI SELF CONTROL TECHNIQUES:
The Stall & Redirect Technique
The Transition Technique
The Truth Technique

DIRECT WITH BODY LANGUAGE:
Open Arms
Crossed Arms
Fingers Interlaced, Leaning on Knees
Glace at Watch
Nodding
Pointing
Mirroring
Smiling

2. REDIRECT

Indirect Redirection - Present
Indirect Redirection - Absent
Direct Statement of Validation
Direct Statement of Consequences
Interjection
Relation - Self
Relation - Consequence
Removal - Subject
Removal - Self
The Sandwich
Intermission

3. CORRECT

Indirect Corrections: Time Out, Correction by Proxy, Correction by Example, Writing Task, Refer to Higher Authority

Direct Corrections: Time In, Direct Verbal, Direct verbal with Consequence

Mixed Corrections: Loss of Privileges, Community service

4. REWARD

Release of Pressure
Reversal of Correction
Material Reward
Theoretical Reward
Privilege Reward
Honor/Award
Increased Responsibility
Special Event
Personal Commendation/Praise

RUNNING TASKS:

1. BLI and Behavior Observation, Documentation & Analysis – Others
2. BLI and Behavior Observation, Documentation & Analysis – Self
3. Reward Brainstorming

PRIMARY PHILOSOPHIES:

Prevention over Correction
Humans are Animals
Friendly Never Friends
Never Threaten; Always Predict
Do Not Take Rejection Personally
Be neither Predator nor Prey

www.preemptive.info

If you find yourself lacking motivation or encouragement in order to stay consistent in your application of PBT, I have selected some excellent quotes from influential people that you might find inspirational. Pick a couple of them that you like and write them on little sticky notes and post them near your desk, computer, bedside table, mirror or anywhere else where you'll see them on a regular basis.

"I believe that we learn by practice. Whether it means to learn to dance by practicing dancing or to learn to live by practicing living, the principles are the same. In each, it is the performance of a dedicated precise set of acts, physical or intellectual, from which comes shape of achievement, a sense of one's being; a satisfaction of spirit."
~Martha Graham

"Practice is the hardest part of learning, and training is the essence of transformation."
~Ann Voskamp

"Tomorrow's victory is today's practice."
~Chris Bradford

"For the things we have to learn before we can do them, we learn by doing them."
~Aristotle

"You are what you practice most."
~Richard Carlson

"Practice makes the master."
~Patrick Rothfuss

"Practice doesn't make perfect. Practice reduces the imperfection."
~Toba Beta

"Love and magic have a great deal in common. They enrich the soul, delight the heart. And they both take practice."
~Nora Roberts

"Knowledge is of no value unless you put it into practice."
~Anton Chekhov

Good ideas are not adopted automatically. They must be driven into practice with courageous patience.
~Hyman Rickover

"It is a mistake to think that the practice of my art has become easy to me. I assure you,

dear friend, no one has given so much care to the study of composition as I. There is scarcely a famous master in music whose works I have not frequently and diligently studied."
~Wolfgang Amadeus Mozart

Mozart's quote sets the stage for our next section, which is an index of resources that will help you understand, apply and practice the principles of PBT. Use these resources - learn from them like Mozart learned from the masters he studied.

As much as I would like to tell you that this book is all that you will need in order to make Preemptive Behavior Therapy a part of your life and the life of the kids you work with; it's not. I developed these principles after years of personal study of people in the field that I admired, and of course decades of actual practice. But I am still in training.

Despite my busy schedule I am still in school; I still seek out education, criticism and encouragement and this is something that I will never stop doing. Even though I created PBT I am still discovering new ways to effectively use it and new principles and their related tweaks that might not have been voiced or written before.

As you progress with your knowledge of body language and your consistent application of PBT, you too will discover tricks and tweaks that apply only to you and the people you work with. This is completely normal and recommended. After all; we are humans and as such very little can be applied universally to everyone.

Each person's specific body language and related quirks will be slightly different, their histories will be different, and with your help, their futures will be different too. So if you discover better ways of applying the principles of PBT, then I encourage you to do so, and I strongly recommend that you write about it. I'd love to hear from you!

RESOURCES & SUPPLEMENTAL INFORMATION

BODY LANGUAGE

The works of Albert Mehrabian:
Silent messages: Implicit communication of emotions and attitudes.
Decoding of Inconsistent Communications
Inference of Attitudes from Nonverbal Communication in Two Channels

The works of Joe Navarro
Reserved Behaviors in the Study of Nonverbal Communications
What Every Body is Saying
Louder than Words
The Power of Body Language
Body Language of the Hands

The works of Susan Weinschenk
Your Hand Gestures are Speaking for You
100 Things Every Presenter Needs To Know About People

The works of Ray Crozier
Understanding the Blush
Coping with Shyness and Social Phobia
Blushing and the Social Emotions: The Self Unmasked
Understanding Shyness: Psychological Perspectives
Individual Learners: Personality Differences in Education

The works of David Matsumoto, Ph.D.
Nonverbal Communication Science and Applications

The works of Nick Morgan, Ph.D.
How to Read Body Language
Power Cues: The Subtle Science of Leading Groups, Persuading Others, and Maximizing Your Personal Impact

The works of Susan Constantine
The Complete Idiot's Guide to Reading Body Language

The works of Robert Phipps
Body Language - It's What You Don't Say That Matters

ANIMAL BEHAVIOR & COMMUNICATION

Carol Gurney - The Gurney Institute of Animal Communication
http://www.gurneyinstitute.com/

The works of John Lyons
Bringing Up Baby
Lyons on Horses: John Lyons' Proven Conditioned-Response Training Program
Communicating with Cues: The Rider's Guide to Training and Problem Solving

The works of Karen Anderson
Hear All Creatures! The Journey of an Animal Communicator

The works of Tim Link
Wagging Tales: Every Animal has a Tale

The works of Penelope Smith
Animal Talk: Interspecies Telepathic Communication
When Animals Speak: Techniques for Bonding with Animal Companions

William Hillix, Duane Rumbaugh
Animal Bodies, Human Minds: Ape, Dolphin, and Parrot Language Skills

MOTHER TERESA'S MISSION
www.motherteresa.org

PROFESSIONAL BOUNDARIES WORKING WITH KIDS

The works of Frank Cooper
Professional Boundaries in Social Work and Social Care: A Practical Guide to

Understanding, Maintaining and Managing Your Professional Boundaries

Laura Hoyano, Caroline Keenan
Child Abuse: Law and Policy across Boundaries

The works of Jane Adams
Boundary Issues: Using Boundary Intelligence to Get the Intimacy You Want and the Independence You Need in Life, Love, and Work

CAREGIVERS OF TROUBLED CHILDREN

The works of David Rettew
Child Temperament: New Thinking about the Boundary between Traits and Illness

The works of Larry Brendtro
Re-Educating Troubled Youth

The works of Lawrence Diller
Should I Medicate My Child? Sane Solutions for Troubled Kids with-and-without Psychiatric Drugs

The works of Daniel A. Hughes
Building the Bonds of Attachment: Awakening Love in Deeply Troubled Children

Carolyn Webster-Stratton, Martin Herbert
Troubled Families-Problem Children: Working with Parents: A Collaborative Process

The works of Carole Sutton
Helping Families with Troubled Children: A Preventive Approach

The works of John C. Coleman
Working with Troubled Adolescents

Another additional resource is the Preemptive Behavior Therapy website found at www.preemptive.info. The site will be continually expanding its features, including robust forums, articles and papers, commentary, blog posts and materials such as the PBT At-a-Glance found in this chapter, as well as downloadable tracking sheets and more. We will also be featuring workbooks and study sheets in the near future.

In addition, I plan to provide details about the upcoming release of my second book, which will guide readers and PBT practitioners through animal communication and how it relates to the principles of PBT.

At some point soon we will also offer training and certification programs to practitioners of PBT. This will allow professionals to gain certification in order to demonstrate their knowledge and proficiency of the principles of this program. In order to take part in this program when it becomes available, please send me an email through the contact form on the site and indicate your interest. Conferences, seminars and comprehensive training materials will be available in 2015.

If you have ideas or suggestions for additional resources that practitioners of PBT may find useful, please contact me via www.preemptive.info and I will be happy to discuss them with you for possible inclusion online or in an upcoming edition of this or other texts about PBT.

10 DUAL FACETED PERSPECTIVE

A few years ago I found myself itching to get something out of me. I found an outlet in a pen and pad of paper and began writing down notes of my thoughts and ideas. These quickly developed into informal short stories, essays, collections of ideas, etc. Eventually I tried to put all of these writings together into something that I could make better sense of and share with others who might find the information helpful in their personal lives or careers.

I had no idea what I wanted to do with these writings; I just knew that something called me to get what was inside of me out. I felt like I was blessed to have discovered and refined practices that achieved significant success for me and brought many kids out of a long slide into darkness.

The trouble is that I am not a writer. I am a communicator by trade and by essence, but for me this communication lives in the realm of present, direct interactions. Whether speaking to a crowd or a small child, I am able to articulate my ideas clearly and with significant effect when combined with deliberate body language and the energies that only come with direct personal engagement.

But when it comes to writing, I don't have a living animal or person in front of me to impart this energy to, and so instead it builds up and explodes on the page, resulting in masses of concise thoughts but with no concise ordering.

So I sent my work to American writer and editor Russ Hudson, who puzzled over it for weeks before getting back to me. His response was short;

Preemptive Behavior Therapy

"Seems to me like there's a book trying to escape from this mess, as the overall message of your work is larger than the sum of its parts."

And that's how this book was born.

But there's a lot more to the story. As it turns out, Russ spent his childhood and adolescence as one of the kids that this book discusses. While I had been on the frontlines working with kids to keep them safe and help them grow, Russ was on the backlines; living on the streets, in shelters, group homes, institutions, etc.

Given up at age 3 by his then 18 year old mother, Russ was adopted by a family that turned out to be abusive. He began running away from this home at age 8 and left for the last time at age 11, never to return. This put him on the streets of Portland, Maine, United States, where he stayed in homeless shelters until the State eventually realized they couldn't have such a young boy running about.

A court order placed Russ in State custody and remanded him to a foster home that only lasted for 6 months. From there Russ was sent to Good-Will Hinckley near Fairfield, Maine. "Hinckley," as the place is called locally, is a large private boarding school for boys and girls. He was there on and off for 2 years, occasionally running away until at age 13 he went back to live on the streets.

The next few years continued in this same sort of trend; Russ found himself at the Atrium House, the Halcyon House, Youth Alternatives, the Lighthouse Shelter, the Shaw House, a foster home, the Day One group home in Hollis, the Your Choice house in Hallowell, and several stints in the Maine Youth Detention Center - a correctional facility for kids.

Russ spent much of the time in between each of these places on the run; hiding out, being taken in by random people, living under bridges and in tents in the woods, etc. He told me that at each new place the State would send him he would earnestly try to make it work. But ultimately, many of the programs were staffed by under-qualified, neglectful or even abusive workers, and the behavioral systems in place were rarely effective. After a few weeks or a few months, Russ would run away and try to live on his own for as long as he could before getting picked up by the police again.

All of this experience means that Russ has lived in and participated in many of the traditional behavioral programs and settings that are normally available to kids in his and similar situations. Russ was placed in points-based programs, family teaching models, correctional models, farm-based models, real-life based models, voting based models (MYC), credits-based models, etc.

So here was a man who had lived on the other side of the coin, so to speak. His insight into my work was extremely unique, but the uncanniness doesn't end there.

During his years living with his original adoptive family, Russ gained a significant amount of experience working with animals. The adoptive family lived and worked on one of the state's largest farms, which meant that Russ spent most of his early years working with cows, horses, chickens, turkeys, dogs and other domestic animals. And because the farm was exceptionally rich with wildlife, Russ also spent a great deal of time observing, tracking, managing, trapping and hunting animals on the property. This included coyotes, fox, deer, moose, beavers, eagles, vultures, porcupines, raccoons and more.

Fortunately for him, Russ was a smart kid and was incredibly resourceful. He entered college at age 17 while living on the streets of the State capital and pursued a degree in Animal Science. He then traveled out to the American west to train dogs for high altitude and other rescue work. He worked in shelters and veterinary clinics from an early age, and eventually managed the private riding stables of a wealthy businessman in Acadia National Park. During this time Russ worked with trail horses that were often unruly and poorly trained. He also once bred a fine litter of AKC Labrador Retrievers.

When I learned all of this about Russ, I just had to laugh. It's funny how the universe works, isn't it? It just so happened that the one writer I had chosen to submit my work to had extensive, working practical knowledge of animal communication. And even more importantly, he had seen my work through the eyes of a child. He was the child that I am here for today, and he was the child that prompted you to pick up this book and start reading.

Because of his experience, Russ understood the message I was trying to elicit with my work, and here it is, right now, in your hands. We hope this holistic approach helps you make a difference in the lives of children who need you.

www.ingramcontent.com/pod-product-compliance
Lightning Source LLC
Chambersburg PA
CBHW060016050426
42448CB00012B/2777